A   s any
tea   their
stu   t the
rea   that
so   ative,
enj

ning,
lation

Rachel Jones is one of the most respected teachers on Twitter and in the world of educational blogging. This book shows just why that respect is deserved: it is practical, grounded, warm and human. The book, in fact, is Rachel!

Rachel celebrates the 'teacher geek' whose passion and enthusiasm for their subject, and for learning (both their own and others'), motivates and inspires them. She shows how to 'create sparks of interest that light the fires of learning', sometimes through the use of ICT, sometimes by using what you can pick up in the charity or pound shop.

Rachel's advice is to be brave, take risks and tweak and adapt resources (including our environment, images, sound and music) creatively

so that they serve as a 'hook for learning'. By being flexible and imaginative we can put a new spin on things, think differently and adopt a new perspective, while still being ourselves. This book will make a difference to teachers.

Jill Berry, education consultant, former head teacher

I love this book and I want to do everything that Rachel Jones describes. I want my graph theory class to build graphs out of marshmallows and BBQ skewers and we'll do that. Amidst all the pressures that teachers face, of marking and administration and everything else that we do, it's easy to forget the fun we can and should have as teachers. Reading Rachel's book reminded me of the fun of being a student and of the fun that I can have as a teacher. Within a short space of time, my copy will be dog eared and sticky-noted with lots of marginal notes describing the things that have worked for me and the things I want to try next.

Dr James W. Anderson, associate dean, University of Southampton

From vibrators to vibratos (yes, you read that right), Rachel takes the reader on a fascinating tour of her pedagogic world in this how-to guide with a difference. Be you an 'analogue geek' or a 'digital geek' teacher, there's plenty here for you to think about, try and learn to enhance your classroom practice. Although some of the ideas in the book are not for the faint-hearted or those teaching within a highly regimented school (get out while you still can), each chapter brings gifts for the beginner geek.

This is a permission-giving book whose core message is 'recapture your classroom'. It won't be to everyone's taste and nor should it be. But if you've ever discerned the inner desire to draw on desks or wondered wistfully what it would be like to write on windows, this is most definitely the book for you.

Keven Bartle, head teacher, Canons High School

TEACHER GEEK

Because life's too short for worksheets

Rachel Jones

Crown House Publishing Limited
www.crownhouse.co.uk

First published by
Crown House Publishing Limited
Crown Buildings, Bancyfelin, Carmarthen, Wales, SA33 5ND, UK
www.crownhouse.co.uk

and

Crown House Publishing Company LLC
6 Trowbridge Drive, Suite 5, Bethel, CT 06801, USA
www.crownhousepublishing.com

All images © Rachel Jones with the exception of cover images © Rawpixel - fotolia.com, sticky note image
© Picture-Factory - fotolia.com, images page 1 © okinawakasawa - fotolia.com, page 6-7 © Rawpixel - fotolia.
com, page 9 © PiXXart Photography - fotolia.com, page 16 © korurumod - fotolia.com, page 17 © K.- P. Adler
- fotolia.com, pages 19-22 © iuneWind - fotolia.com, pages 24-25 © Igor Mojzes - fotolia.com, page 41 © Sergey
Nivens - fotolia.com, pages 50-51 © Rawpixel - fotolia.com, page 53 © Bastos - fotolia.com, page 54 © roo -
fotolia.com, page 56 © kuco - fotolia.com, pages 64-65 © Rawpixel - fotolia.com, page 66 © Alexandra
Thompson - fotolia.com, page 67 © naxaso - fotolia.com, page 73 © dip - fotolia.com, page 76-77 © Rawpixel,
© olshole, © rea_molko - fotolia.com, page 82 © olshole, © rea_molko - fotolia.com, page 89 © Bastetamon -
fotolia.com, pages 90-91 © Rawpixel - fotolia.com, pages 94-95 © Luis Louro - fotolia.com, page 99 © Gina
Sanders - fotolia.com, pages 104-105 © Rawpixel - fotolia.com, pages 106-107 © Nomad_Soul - fotolia.com,
pages 118-119 © twixx - fotolia.com, pages 120-121 © Rawpixel - fotolia.com, pages 122-123 © katusha161107
- fotolia.com, page 126 © Kuzmick - fotolia.com, page 137 © destina, © traza - fotolia.com.

British Library Cataloguing-in-Publication Data

A catalogue entry for this book is available from the British Library.

Print ISBN 978-184590986-4
Mobi ISBN 978-184590957-9
ePub ISBN 978-184590988-8
ePDF ISBN 978-184590989-5

LCCN 2015942005

Printed and bound in the UK by
Gomer Press, Llandysul, Ceredigion

This book is for my family, who had to put up with me being the worst teenager ever. This book is also for my boys, Finley and Frazer, who make every day an adventure. Finally, this book is for the boy, Matt, who makes me think a lot but smile more.

CONTENTS

Foreword by Doug Lemov

A few years ago I watched a teacher step into an anxiety dream. She was interviewing for a job at a school and had been asked to teach a sample lesson. I was spending the day with the principal and so joined him to observe the lesson. Her topic was the water cycle and she had prepped a few slides and a short video, I think, on her laptop to get things rolling. I say, 'I think' because the projector and her laptop wouldn't sync or the bulb didn't work. I don't remember which, exactly, but the tech did as the tech sometimes does – which is to say it did not work. So really, who knows what she'd planned. But there she stood, as if in a bad dream in front of 30 or so 11-year-olds, not to mention the school's principal and a few fellow teachers, with 30 minutes in which to win a job and her lesson plan melting faster than butter in the sun.

But of course, she was a teacher and when it comes to crises, a teacher is used to that sort of thing. Hardly a day goes by when a teacher does not have to adapt what she is doing to the absurd, the froward, the unpredictable, the inspired, or the serendipitous. The mere non-functionality of a slide show was, frankly, just another day at work. She picked up a water bottle off the desk, crumpled a sheet of paper – that was the cloud, obviously – and proceeded to model the water cycle. I still don't know what was on that laptop of hers, but it couldn't have been much better than the impromptu demo and discussion she pulled off.

I thought of that teacher when I started reading this book because Rachel Jones delights in the problem-solving aspects of the classroom. Problem solving is one of the most developed and least acknowledged skills of the typical teacher and it's a skill Rachel embraces, celebrates even. But Rachel is not a typical teacher. She is a teacher who likes to relish the possibilities. As we say of some of our most accomplished teachers, the ones who seem to rise above when things look trickiest, she loves trouble. She wants to open your eyes to the world of solutions and opportunities that exist in the humble settings of your classroom, achieved by your unexpected decision to write on the floor, say. Or to redesign your discussion. To plan a slide show. Or to ditch the slide show and make a cloud out of a piece of paper. In her vison, and more importantly in this book, the possibilities are endless.

And beyond the myriad ideas she proposes, maybe the most valuable thing is the irrepressible sense of optimism that pervades her book. And ethos of can-do. Whether or not every solution she proposes is for you, the practice of looking at problems as opportunities for creative solutions is rather exhilarating, and that is the killer app from this book. If you see it a certain way, problem solving is one of the best parts of the job. When you start to think that way you will be a teacher geek and there will be nothing you cannot conquer.

Doug Lemov, managing director, Uncommon Schools,
author of *Teach Like a Champion 2.0, Practice Perfect*
and *Reading Reconsidered*

Acknowledgements

I would like to thank everyone at Crown House Publishing and Independent Thinking. You all rock a lot. I would also like to thank my school, King Edward VI in Southampton, for being supportive and encouraging. I would not have been able to write this book without the encouragement of my #nurture team and my friends, so thank you and massive love to all. In particular, @ChocoTzar has had the patience of a saint helping me. Thank you also to all my students, past and present, for shaping how I think and how I teach – it has been a real privilege to work with you all.

Introduction

The last thing you need is someone else telling you that what you do in your classroom isn't right, isn't good enough, or isn't what Ofsted want. You don't need me to tell you that your lesson lacks whizz or va va voom. I know what it feels like to rush from one end of a school to the other for a lesson mysteriously timetabled in a former cupboard where the atmosphere is anything less than inspiring. I know what it feels like to have a head of department (or member of senior management) who can't see beyond the data or the most recent educational trend.

Here are some facts about the majority of teachers:

- Teachers work hard. Really hard. Much to the bafflement of their friends and family, and probably everyone else who finishes work and then goes home with no more work to do.

- Teaching can be the most rewarding job in the world but also the most draining. It can sometimes feel like it takes more effort than one of those mountainous ascents in the Tour de France.

- Teachers' self-worth is based on the outcomes of their students, yet at the same time we accept that in many cases we are fighting a tough battle.

- Most teachers do a good job most of the time and an outstanding job some of the time. Most of us also teach lessons that we know are not good enough. But it doesn't mean we give up trying.

- Most schools lack the money to buy essentials, never mind much else, so teachers buy their own classroom tools. I sometimes wonder if teachers are actually keeping pound shops afloat (we should all certainly get share options).

- All teachers have produced dreadful hand-outs, PowerPoints and other resources – the sort that we do not brag about on blogs or at TeachMeets.

- All teachers sometimes feel they are not doing well enough. And that's without the exam boards moving the boundaries.

If this sounds familiar then I want you to know that you are not alone. You could have a chat in any staffroom up or down the country and find a sense of camaraderie. For every teacher who wins a teaching award there are millions who would never even consider nominating himself or herself. And for every education blogger there are thousands who think they have nothing of value to say.

So stop. Stop now.

There is nothing wrong with what you are doing, but by making a few minor tweaks you could make your life a whole lot easier and gain the rapt attention of your class. I think that the best teachers are 'geeks'. Not in the derogatory sense that the word has been used in the past, but in the sense that we celebrate our enthusiasm for our subjects and for learning. Teacher geeks are a unique breed. They get excited over new stationery, they enjoy learning new things and, most importantly, they enjoy passing on their passion to the learners in their classroom. Being a 'geek teacher' is all about celebrating a real love of teaching and learning, with a slight leaning towards embedding using IT in lessons. This book shows you how to blend edu-geeky analogue and digital teaching techniques, alongside suggestions on how to inspire your students and revitalise your practice. So edu-geeks unite. Let's make our lessons better and make the geek, chic.

Passion is a hallmark of being a geek teacher, and part of that passion is about seeing those you teach do well and achieve. Goodness knows it is almost impossible to measure learning or progress, but for me there is some weight in that feeling of achievement when your lesson is going well. Dare I say it, lessons should be engaging. They should create sparks of interest that light the flames of learning, so that when the bell goes at the end of the lesson you can still hear your students buzzing about what they have learned as they walk down the corridor. This isn't going to happen in every lesson, but when it does it is pure magic and something to be treasured. Remember that progress looks different for every learner. For some even picking up a pen and writing a few lines can be monumental; for others you might be constantly running around to find more challenging work and struggling to keep pace with their appetite for learning. Being a geek teacher is about having the patience to make learning accessible and challenging for all, and sparking an interest in every child.

> **Passion is a hallmark of being a geek teacher,** and part of that passion is about seeing those you teach do well and achieve.

You are the teacher to every child in your classroom, and the juggling act required to make learning accessible as well as challenging means you need to be adaptable, flexible and willing to take risks in developing your practice. It is not good enough to hand out the same worksheets year after year. You are asking your learners to take a massive risk in trusting you and opening themselves up to potential failure. As the grown-up in the room, you need to role model what positive risk taking looks like and deal with failure in a way that will help the learners to see it as part of the learning process. Being a geek teacher is all about seeing your students as individuals, and helping them to achieve their potential and, importantly, being comfortable with being a learner yourself.

You have nothing to lose and everything to gain by trying out a few new ideas in your classroom. The best lesson I've ever learned is always to have a plan B up your sleeve. This applies especially when using technology or when you are reliant on forces you cannot control. A back-up plan means there will always be meaningful learning in our classrooms, but we will also earn the respect of those we teach because we have their interests at the forefront of our planning.

We are all at the mercy of serendipity sometimes. You can't expect a class to react to something in the same way they did the day, the week or the term before. A group that once loved role play might now quake at the idea. A class that worked well in groups might not if it's near lunchtime and their tummies are rumbling. Children can be volatile and unpredictable, but one thing needs to be constant – and that is you. You need to be consistent, fair and present. The students need to see that you care and are invested in them. If we can agree on that then we are on the same metaphorical page.

> **You need to be consistent, fair and present.**

So, are you feeling brave?

In this book I want to show you how to use techniques or technologies that you may already use, but in an original way. Put a new spin on things. Think a little differently. Be yourself but from a new perspective. To do this I would like you to think about these points when you are planning, in the classroom or even marking:

- It is easier to ask for forgiveness than permission. By this I don't mean do something ridiculous that will get you suspended or featured in the local press. If you are trying something new remember you are a competent professional – you don't always need to seek approval from those around or above you.

- Pursue new activities in your classroom. Be OK with taking risks and be brave enough to call it when they are not working out.

- Seek out opportunities to work with others and try to say yes as often as possible to prospects that come your way. Teach this open-mindedness to your students too.

- Use technology where appropriate. Accept that it won't always work and be comfortable with your students being more skilled than you.

- Don't accept the view that good pedagogy is constrained by subject or age. Some of the most inspiring teaching practice I have seen has been in the primary phase, but it adapts perfectly well for use in secondary and beyond.

- Be yourself. Share some of yourself with your class. You are not a teaching robot; you are a human being. Know your learners and plan with them at the centre of everything.

IN THIS CHAPTER:

- Rethinking your classroom – swapping old for new.

- Using traditional analogue teaching methods in unusual ways.

- Adopting digital methods.

Chapter 1
OLD FOR NEW
beyond charity shop thinking

Being a geek teacher means taking real pleasure in engaging your learners by using resources in creative ways. You can take a few elements and rework them to produce something different. Not only are you creating something new from long-established classroom materials, like worksheets, but you are also rethinking your students' attitudes to learning and their potential outcomes.

Being a geeky teacher involves doing something different with our primary materials. This allows us to consider how we might have once interpreted those materials, how the students might understand them and, most importantly, it highlights the cultural context of those materials and the learning in our classrooms.

For example, if you have a tub of modelling clay don't just use it for play modelling as that was just its intended purpose. You could, for example, have children sculpt their identity in PSHE or model their learning from the lesson. Similarly you might have balloons that you could redeploy in your classroom for the purpose of learning. Rethink the objects and resources you have access to, and give them an educational purpose. Never do this just for the sake of doing it, but do it because it will make your teaching more effective or enhance the students' learning.

I'm sure it will come as no surprise to teachers that the resources we see as having meaning and value are often not held in the same regard by our students. This gives us the opportunity to think honestly about the materials we bring into the learning environment. Considering them from the students' perspective should be something we do as part of best practice, but this may often fall aside in the bustle of lesson preparation and marking. I am certainly not advocating that your lessons or activities should be resource driven; in fact, anything but. However, resources are part and parcel of teaching so it is essential to take the time to consider what we are using and why.

This is particularly important when considering the cultural context of learning materials. I once taught on a university course on the history of sexuality (never before have I said the word 'vagina' so much). For a class considering the feminist view of sex toys, I had borrowed a Victorian hand-powered vibrator from a local museum. It was certainly phallic, but none of the students realised what it was at first. They passed it around, turning the handle to make it slightly vibrate. One student even sniffed it. At this point I wasn't sure if I should tell them or try to pretend it was something more innocent. But, no, one student then identified it. The object was dropped on the floor and the entire class descended into chaos as the previously innocuous looking historical object was revealed to be a sex toy. I'm not sure I had considered the full potential impact in advance, but it is certainly one of my more memorable lessons! We then went on to study relevant feminist texts, but the interaction with the resource/object as a hook for learning (rather than just an object in a display case) did go some way to creating some very interesting written work. I have never forgotten this lesson and the power that using objects in the classroom can have.

ANALOGUE TEACHING

With the Victorian vibrator in mind, I am first of all going to ask you to rework some analogue elements of your classroom. For me, analogue teaching is, very simply, everything that isn't digital – that might be your planner, mark-book, hand-outs or task-sheets or even sticky notes.

ENCOURAGING A STATIONERY FETISH

Let's start with the humble sticky note. I think all teachers have a stationery fetish. We secretly relish the back-to-school shop for stocking up on colourful gel pens and bright new pencil cases. Many teachers have quite a stash of sticky notes. Not only are they useful for leaving notes (in bright pink they are more difficult to ignore than an email!), but they can also be put to work in the classroom during plenaries or even as ways of reporting learning in activities.

But how about trying out some of these ideas?

Much of the work I do at the beginning of term is about creating a classroom where each student feels safe and valued, and a class or tutor project to create sticky note art is a great ice-breaker. Each student could have a sticky note to draw on or write about themselves which you then make into a mural on the wall.[1]

Sticky notes can also be used to make a pledge wall. This link shows an example from a school that was produced after the 2007 London bombings.[2] The pledge here is obviously one of solidarity against terrorism and a show of collectivism. Pledge walls are a lovely visual way of asserting the class or school identity at a time of potential upheaval. The students could also offer to pledge a small sum to a relevant charity – for example, I have seen pledge walls used to champion environmental issues or to support charities like Amnesty International. They make great temporary displays, but they can also be kept for a long time – if you have the patience to make sure the sticky notes don't fall off! I can easily imagine the pledge wall as a focus in a school reception area or hall for an anti-bullying or e-safety campaign that students have worked on collaboratively.

So let's not just think of the humble sticky note as being only for the exit ticket scribbles. Let's put it to more creative use. Just google something like 'sticky note display' and you will find all kinds of inspiration – like this amazing piece of artwork.[3]

BLACKOUT TEXT/OLD BOOKS

Another way of reusing something old in your classroom is to blackout words in a text. This has been used prolifically in the form of blackout poetry.[4] Teachers have also begun to use this imaginative approach in the classroom, often using old books bought at car boot sales as a creative writing prompt.[5]

A modification to using blackout work can be seen in the following key words template, that I created for my students, which uses words cut out from newspapers and magazines.

---

1 For an example see: http://artjunction.org/art-on-a-post-it-note/.
2 See http://media.creativebloq.futurecdn.net/sites/creativebloq.com/files/images/2012/11/peacewall3.jpg.
3 For an example see: http://blog.catchmyparty.com/wp-content/uploads/2010/09/post-it-note-art.jpg.
4 For an example see: http://library.movlic.com/CheckItOut/12/NowTrending.
5 For an example see: http://davidblackmore.blogspot.co.uk/2010/12/development-of-self-help-at-schwatrz.html.

tionalism INDIVIDUALISM world. culture

what's SOUGHT IDENTITY a

risk more EFFECTIVE

Maffesoli

identity punk Culture BASED W

Keep are

NEO-TRIBES FOCUS W

Research strength magic

world McKay THIS

MEDIA argue

GLOBALISATION to shows far

ARGUMENT is still indiv

of INE

thi

uctural sociologica

MIX cccs MODERN EVALUATE ju

Sociology SATURATED

importan

ument subcultures wh

Mi

Macro IS of RAVE analysis aga

A AND tell LIVING likely they

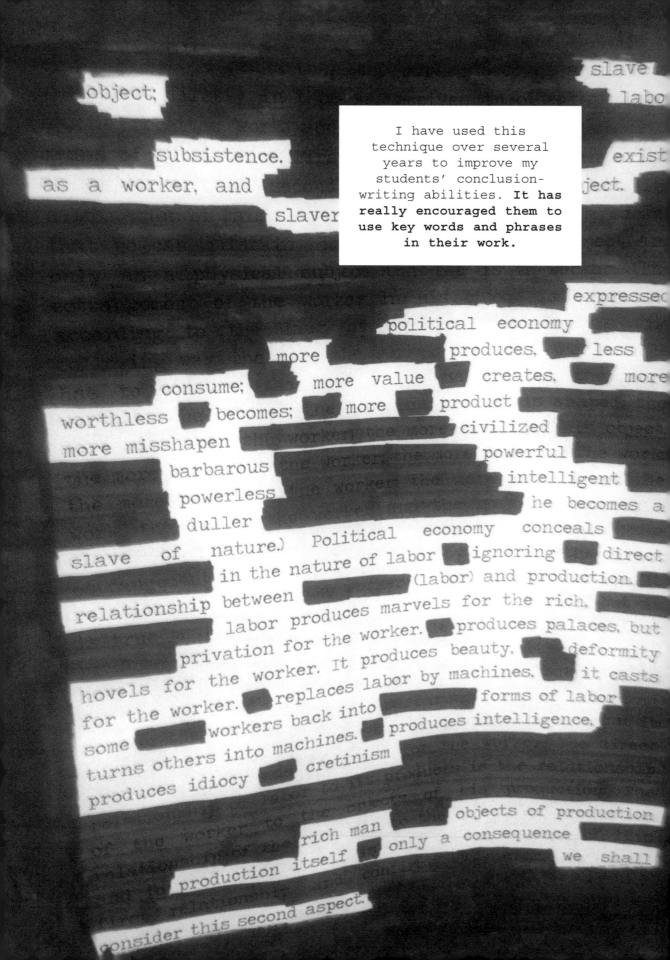

object;

subsistence.

as a worker, and

slaver

slave

labo

exist

ject.

I have used this technique over several years to improve my students' conclusion-writing abilities. **It has really encouraged them to use key words and phrases in their work.**

expressed

political economy

more   produces,   less

consume;   more value   creates,   more

worthless   becomes;   more   product

more misshapen   civilized

barbarous   powerful

powerless   intelligent

he becomes a

duller

slave of nature.) Political economy conceals

in the nature of labor   ignoring   direct

relationship between   (labor) and production.

labor produces marvels for the rich,

privation for the worker.   produces palaces, but

hovels for the worker. It produces beauty,   deformity

for the worker.   replaces labor by machines,   it casts

some   workers back into   forms of labor

turns others into machines.   produces intelligence,

produces idiocy   cretinism

objects of production

rich man   only a consequence

production itself   we shall

consider this second aspect.

I have used this technique over several years to improve my students' conclusion-writing abilities. It has really encouraged them to use key words and phrases in their work. The activity also helps them to remember other important knowledge points, such as the names of theorists, as they are unable to complete the task without an understanding of different theorists' ideas and observations. This is a perfect example of an activity that not only develops literacy skills but also improves the retention of factual information.

You could also produce blackout introductions or even sections of a body of text (e.g. an essay) to force learners to slow down and really consider the words the writer is using to express their ideas. In order to reach the top grade boundaries, some exam boards expect students to use evaluative language. This technique can be a creative way to reinforce the habit so by the time they get to the exam it has become second nature.

I think it is important to leave space in your lessons for the students to be creative. Too often we are pressurised into making learning mechanical and teacher centred. It is not the case that a creative activity is a pointless one if it doesn't have an obvious meaningful outcome. Just giving students some space in the day to engage with their learning in a different way can help them to make connections within the work that would not have been possible through a mock-exam or worksheet. Remember, some of the greatest scientific discoveries of the last few centuries have come about through individuals or groups working in a creative way, so allow some space for creativity when you are planning lessons.

> Remember, some of the greatest scientific discoveries of the last few centuries have come about through individuals or groups working in a creative way, **so allow some space for creativity when you are planning lessons.**

COLLAGE

Collaging is a skill much neglected in the classroom. It gives younger children valuable practice at refining their fine motor skills and older ones the opportunity to have some quiet thinking time about a topic before putting pen to paper. I remember happy hours spent chopping up magazines and newspapers when I was little, and I have taken what I found to be a valuable experience for expressing myself into the classroom.

So, how should you go about this? Most schools have a pile of old magazines in the staffroom. Snaffle them away (you might need to ask the librarian if they have control of old magazines) and the next time you start a topic, ask the children to get chopping and make a collage of their initial ideas. Alternatively, ask parents to collect old magazines and weekend supplements for you to use in the classroom.

Watching the students cutting out images and developing ideas to make a pictorial representation of the topic is a joy. By necessity they have to learn to cooperate with each other, and the collaborative work they produce can be an excellent starter for lessons. For example, you could begin by showing them their collage and saying, 'Well, last lesson we thought this. Can you tell me how your thinking has changed in three sentences/ adjectives?' This can provide a starting point for many conversations and, more importantly, reflections on the learning that has taken place. As an added bonus, if you put the work on the wall your classroom will be a celebration of the children's work, as it should be.

RECYCLING

Some objects can be upcycled to make for stimulating and engaging lessons. Many teachers buy their own supplies to take into school, but one way to spend less is to use pound shops or hunt for useful items in charity shops or jumble sales.[6]

I find reusing old books really satisfying because the children use them in some very interesting ways. One technique that is particularly successful is to use a book as a background to an artwork linked to topic or subject work. It is even better if the children are working on a page from a book which is related to the subject they have been studying – for example, drawing a volcano on an old map or geography textbook, or visualising Boo from *To Kill A Mocking Bird* on a page of writing from the novel. Once the children have been artistic with old books, pages can be photocopied and blown up to make into wall displays.

You might also consider using second-hand books in more radical ways. This is not for the book-vandalism-squeamish, but cutting books up to find key paragraphs of interest can work really well for encouraging children to identify writing styles, literary techniques or genres. Use the cut-ups as a

---

6 Thanks to @wallaceisabella for her thoughts on this: Isabella Wallace, Poundstore Pedagogy – Inspiration in the Aisles, *Osiris Educational* (11 March 2013). Available at: http://osiriseducational.co.uk/ osirisblog/blog/poundstore-pedagogy- inspiration-in-the-aisles/.

starting point when thinking about creative writing or even as a fresh approach to controlled assessment work. The point is to get the children, especially those resistant to writing, engaged and curious about books. Let them feel the texture of the pages and smell them – these learners may not have had much contact with old books and this in itself is a stimulating experience.

FANCY DRESS (EVEN FOR BIG KIDS)

Of course, it is not only books that you can find in charity shops. I have an ever-growing box of dressing-up clothes. Oh yes, fancy dress is a crucial tool in a teacher's armoury in the war against boredom and educational ennui! I don't mean custom-made costumes – with imagination old curtains and bedding can easily become a splendid outfit for Achilles from the *Iliad*, or with a bit of gold ribbon an old white sheet can become the robes of the goddess Athena.

I agree with Hywel Roberts that the secret to successful dressing up – which is basically role play or drama – is to never ever call it that.[7] 'Role play' is one of the fastest ways to alienate shy

---

7 Hywel Roberts, Drama, in Rachel Jones (Ed.), *Don't Change the Light Bulbs* (Carmarthen: Crown House Publishing, 2014), pp. 139–141.

children or those who don't enjoy drama as a subject. However, if you use dressing-up clothes with care – with roles planned with specific children in mind – you can usually incorporate a whole class into a production. If you have very timid or nervous children, the costumes can help to transform them.
Alternatively, a directorial role or other key non-speaking part can be valuable in building children's confidence and developing a strengthened class identity.

Remember, don't just reuse objects or do something different for the sake of it. When you try something new make sure the needs of your learners are at its core. Nothing is more important than making a child feel accepted and confident. There is something really satisfying about using old resources in a way that will energise your learners. This desire to transmit a passion for learning is the true hallmark of a teacher geek.

DIGITAL TOOLS

So far we have looked at rethinking analogue objects, but I also want you to reconsider how you use digital tools. I will cover digital applications in more depth in later chapters; however, here I will share some web-based tools that you can use to recycle digital materials that you may already have available, such as old PowerPoints.

In terms of using digital technology in the classroom, my first message is: let your learners make use of the technology they have. There is no point in banning mobile devices under the misapprehension that you are doing the students a favour. A phone in a student's pocket is a wasted learning opportunity. Many teachers, particularly leadership teams, are worried about the misuse of devices, so my second message is: if your students are misusing technology, this is a behaviour management issue, not a problem with the technology itself.

NEARPOD

The first of these genius web tools is called Nearpod. It is a free site which lets you upload an old PowerPoint (don't pretend you don't have any!) and then use various functions to add in assessment for learning opportunities. For example, you can add a class opinion poll, multiple choice questions, a drawing option or even guide learners to a specific website. You are given a class number that your students can use to log in to the site on individual devices. Once logged in you can see their name and their work, so every learner is accountable for what they write. Furthermore, you control the screens of those students who are logged in.

Nearpod is a perfect example of technology that gives students the chance to engage and teachers a unique opportunity to assess their learning at every stage of the lesson. Even better, the results from the lesson are available to you as a spreadsheet so you can really target your help at those who need it most.

This is a total win-win. It is simple and quick to set up, and it has significant impact in the classroom. Teachers – you have the power!

GOOGLE DRIVE

Google Drive is another excellent web tool – in particular, it provides a collaborative environment for students to work on shared files, be they Google Docs or Slides. Google Apps for Education is free and can be set up across the school to integrate a number of features such as Gmail, YouTube, Google Plus, Blogger and Drive, among others.

Google Drive offers both cloud storage and the opportunity for students to work collaboratively on documents. If your class have never done this before they will (I promise) gasp the first time they see a document that they are all working on simultaneously. Experience has taught me that there is usually an obligatory two minutes of them messing about. However, once you point out that you can see exactly who has written or changed what and when in the document, then this will stop.

The power of working in Google Drive is that if the students store their work in a shared folder, then you can see what they are working on and provide vital formative feedback in real time, rather than trying to correct any errors or misconceptions once the work and learning has been done. The students can also comment on each other's work. The essence of collaborative work is that students are not just working on something together, but they are working so that their learning is improving together. By using the comments option in Google Drive, students can use peer feedback to improve their own written skills and that of their fellow students.

Feedback such as, 'This work is brilliant' or 'I like the picture you added', doesn't help other learners to improve and so is of little use. I teach my classes to use FISH feedback,[8] which means they have to make comments that are:

F – Friendly

I – Insightful

S – Specific

H – Helpful

FISH feedback trains a class to see that we can all help each other to learn better. In giving this kind of constructive peer feedback, they are not only honing their own subject knowledge but also learning to be better learners.

Using Google Drive and Google Docs for collaborative work is suitable even for young children. For those teachers with little IT experience, it is relatively easy to get to grips with by playing about for a short while. The social media community of Google+ was particularly helpful to me when I was getting started – just ask for help if you need it. The short-term problems of learning how to use Google Drive are well worth it in terms of the learning gains for your students.

SOCRATIVE

Much can be done to assess students' work using web tools. Socrative allows you to run digital multi-choice and short answer questions, and students' answers are recorded for later use. For me, the best feature of Socrative is that you can run the quiz as a 'space race' so that when students get the answer right they propel a rocket across the screen! Never ever in all my years of teaching have I seen students so competitive and so focused on getting an answer right. Socrative brings an added

---

8 Thanks to @Murphiegirl for her advice on FISH feedback. Check out her blog post on FISH at: Rachael Stevens, FiSH and Tips, *Ed-U-Like* (13 January 2013). Available at: http://edulike.blogspot.co.uk/2013/01/fish-and-tips.html.

dimension to the learning of a class and has more impact than students simply completing a worksheet of questions.

Never kid yourself that the work a student produces has any real meaning if no one sees apart from yourself. A public and wider audience will always have more impact in terms of attainment and learner motivation. In many ways, a shared class activity, using a tool such as Socrative, helps students to pool a sense of urgency and importance around their learning, which may well be lacking for some individuals. Yes, I know that completing a multiple choice quiz will not get a student an A* grade at GCSE, but it may well give them a sense of purposeful learning which can often be missing, especially from underachieving learners.

It is our job as teachers to use tools and methods which motivate and reach *all* the students in our classrooms. Socrative is effective not only in providing challenging questions but also in inspiring participation. In my book, engagement is a step on the path to attainment. Maybe what we need to rethink is not just the resources or tools that we use, but our mindset about what we can achieve as a teacher.

This chapter has been about rethinking the old to make the new by reusing techniques and technologies that you will already have at your disposal. Remember, the focus should always be on planning interventions based on knowing your learners and with the goal of them making progress focused on the learning outcomes. Try something different once a week or every half-term, and see the positive impact that a creative teacher geek approach can have on teaching and learning in your classroom and learning community.

TOP GEEK TIPS

- Charity shops are your friend.

- Allow yourself to be inspired by objects not originally intended for classroom use.

- It doesn't matter if you are using analogue or digital resources. What matters is how they add to the students' learning.

IN THIS CHAPTER:

- Rethinking the classroom environment means doing what is best for your learners.

- Considering all the spaces that you have available as potential learning spaces.

Chapter 2
IT'S YOUR LEARNING ENVIRONMENT
make it mean something

Many teachers rush from one classroom to another, while others have the luxury of staying in the same room all day. Either way, the classroom space is your sanctuary as a professional and a space in which to do really important work with your students. And I don't just mean the academic work, but the work of making them feel welcome, safe and intellectually stimulated. I feel very strongly that we should try to stop thinking of it as being our classroom. It is not your classroom, it is the students' classroom. Being a teacher geek is about being happy with seeing all the available space as a potential learning opportunity.

It is important, therefore, that you see the space not just as somewhere the learning happens, but instead where we celebrate the efforts the children have made, where all children feel safe and valued, where we encourage relationships of mutual trust, and where we use the facilities we have to best help the children learn.

FURNITURE SPACE

Consider your classroom space and what objects you have that the children could use to express their learning. One possibility is for them to write on the tables with board pens (a quick squirt of cleaner and it wipes right off). There is a certain joyous glee in announcing to a class for the first time that they will be writing on the tables. If they have never done so before, trust me, they will take up the offer with zealous enthusiasm.

Rather than a free-for-all, give each child a different coloured pen and get them working as a team. Something that I have found works really well is to use an overhead projector (I bet you still have one lying around) to project an image onto the table,

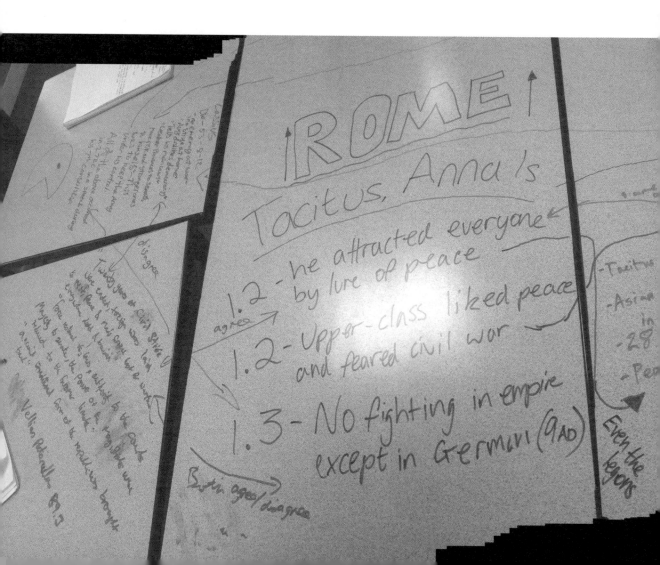

and ask the children to annotate it. You can then take a photograph of their work and either put it in a shared online space, like a virtual learning environment (VLE), or print it out for their books.

Another favourite activity is to have questions written out on the tables when the students come in to the lesson. Then give them a set amount of time to write their answers on the tables. If you search YouTube you will find any number of countdown timers. I quite like using the theme from the TV show *24*, as this makes them write furiously and really focus on the questions they have been asked. When the time is up, I move the students to another table and ask them to see if they can add anything to the answers already there and provide some constructive feedback.

I quite like using the theme from the TV show *24*, as **this makes them write furiously and really focus on the questions they have been asked.**

Depending on what you want the improvement focus of the lesson to be, you can choose different elements for the children to feed back – such as spelling, punctuation, and grammar (SPaG), academic content, use of evaluative language and so on. I have certainly seen that asking for regular feedback on SPaG has improved literacy in my classroom as the children know when they write that they are likely to be given feedback in this area.

While writing on the tables could seem rather anarchic, or perhaps even contrary to the ethos of caring for your school surroundings, in practice the children are meticulous about returning the room to its original state. If they value their classroom environment, there is nothing wrong with making it messy so long as everyone works together to tidy up at the end.

You can buy special paint for tables and walls that can transform them into writing spaces for the children. I have never had the space in my classroom to do this, but think how awesome it would be to have wall space in communal areas to help create a shared school ethos. We hear a lot about school values (and increasingly about how schools transmit 'British values'), so it is beneficial to give students an outlet for expressing what they feel about important issues. It is also an excellent way of demonstrating trust in your learners by implicitly believing in them to use the space responsibly. The funny thing about trusting children is that if you give firm and fair guidelines, the respect becomes two-way. Let's not have schools designed by architects that just look pretty. Let's have schools that have the presence and expression of the children at their heart.

You can also rethink your classroom by using the space to work with paper in a new way. Teachers can feel constrained that children should write in work books or on the ubiquitous A4 lined sheet (don't forget to write the date at the top!). So, how about you raiding your nearest DIY store and getting yourself some bargain roles of plain lining paper. Clear all the tables and chairs to the sides of the room, and roll out a massive line of paper across the length of the classroom – or, better still, down a corridor or across the main hall! You then have enough space to get whole year groups involved in writing for a shared purpose – for example, a graffiti wall of exam advice or reading book suggestions.

Developing writing skills doesn't need to be about keeping neat notes in an exercise book (although this isn't a skill I would recommend anyone neglects). This is about students expressing themselves joyfully through the written language. Watching an entire class, or year group, work on the same piece of paper can be amazing. I would suggest you give each child their own colour pen so you can see who has contributed what, and ask them to initial their work. I have often used this technique as a follow-on to using magazines and other media sources to make a class collage.

> This is about students expressing themselves joyfully through the written language.

WINDOW SPACE

Another physical space that the children can work on is the windows. Most schools are a long way away from having designated glass walls to write on, but windows can work really well. Make sure you buy the right type of pen though – the first time my class did this I bought glass paint pens, which had to be scraped off by a disgruntled member of the premises team. The best type of pens are liquid chalk pens – the same sort used in pubs to write up blackboard menus.

Not only do windows give the children a fabulous space to work, but you can also leave the work on display for future reference. It is a lovely moment when the children see their work from the school playground. I think it is only right that the school, and you as their teacher, give the students the opportunity to display what they have been doing to the wider learning community. Work on windows isn't just a way to encourage writing; it is actually a way of advertising learning.

Here is some work produced by my class. It is valued and I want to show other people. This is a powerful message for children to hear. By sharing their work in this way you are being an advocate for them to improve. You value their work and you want them in your lessons. A total teaching win.

FLOOR SPACE

Another space which has infinite possibilities as a learning tool is the floor. Move all the tables and chairs aside and discover how big the floor space is in your classroom. It's so liberating to have lots of space and to do something different with it. You could play parachute games or ask the children to lie down in the dark and listen to music or stories. What about using the space to put on a drama performance, host a kid's comedy club or open-mike style poetry readings? These are all wonderful things to do to make the experience of the classroom environment unusual, exciting and engaging.

The perfect tool for writing on floors is old-fashioned white chalk. It is miraculous how children will write more when given the opportunity to write on something other than paper. I promise, cross my heart, that the chalk will come off with either a bit of water or a damn good vacuuming. Again, if the children are involved in making a mess in the classroom, then they also need to be involved in clearing it up.

The perfect tool for writing on floors is old-fashioned white chalk. **It is miraculous how children will write more when given the opportunity to write on something other than paper.**

WALL SPACE

How are you using the wall space in your classroom? Most classrooms have display spaces – well, I say that, but some classrooms I've seen have been so bare that they make *Prisoner: Cell Block H* look glamorous. Don't be that teacher who is content with having a blank room. It is our job as teachers to inspire students with interesting spaces that reflect their current learning, not to crush them with mundane surroundings.

DISPLAY BOARDS

If you have wall displays make them accessible and interactive. Spend some time looking for some ideas on Pinterest where there are some really great examples of classroom displays. If you are a secondary teacher, don't be afraid to take inspiration from primary practice, and vice versa.

Here are some suggestions that work really well:

- A stretch and challenge board with articles and ideas to encourage children to aim high. I created one of these at a sixth-form college which included degree-level journal articles. It was brilliant for encouraging wider reading and was much used by the students.

- An award board that focuses on encouraging positive learner behaviours. This is especially powerful if you allow the class to award points rather than it just being a 'teacher's favourite' board. Decide as a class what you want to reward, and then make it public.

- A question board that students can add to. This can then develop into an answer board. Share the path that the learning takes and not just the end product.

- An exit ticket board that students can use as a start point for the next lesson.

Of course, display boards are not the only places that you have for showing work in the classroom – there are also the

Another way to use your classroom walls is to create a word wall.

classroom walls themselves. Some teachers like their classroom to be neat, but I prefer a riotous celebration of the work the children have produced. Show off not only the 'perfect' pieces that you might pull out for an open evening or an Ofsted visit, but also the good efforts and the works in progress. It is right and appropriate for every child to see that their work has a place in the room. Sadly, for many children school is the most secure place in their lives, so it is nurturing for them to feel valued in the room where they spend the majority of their lives.

WORD WALLS

Another way to use your classroom walls is to create a word wall. This is a brilliant activity to reinforce technical vocabulary or specific types of language, such as evaluative phrases. There is no need for you to spend hours making laminated words. Instead, make some time in a lesson to hand out pre-made cards (about revision card sized) and ask the children to write on it a key term, idea or knowledge point. If you give them several cards each then you can select the ones that you would most like them to learn and stick them up on the wall. If you do this every half-term or so then you can build up a word wall that is a working reflection of their learning so far.

You can also use the words in other lesson activities. For example, as a starter, ask students to write down five key words about their learning from the last lesson using the words on the wall. You could then ask them to write sentences on their tables using the key words. Or, as a plenary, ask the children to write down what they have learned using the key words.

This continual reinforcement is an excellent way to teach children to use the technical language that is essential for exam success. A knowledge of subject-specific terms not only helps with understanding a subject, but it also enables students to express their ideas in the expert language used by the teacher. Learning, and the way it is expressed, should not be the private domain of the teacher, but should be shared by all those participating in the learning. You can help your students to do this by exploiting your classroom space to the full.

PLANNING WALLS

A planning wall is a space where you can share your planning with the class. I know this sounds a bit scary, but some of my best planning has come from taking the time to work with students about the types of activities that would best suit the learning. The wealth of ideas that students have gleaned from previous teachers, or from their own outside interests, is an amazing resource. I would never argue with the statement that teachers are the masters of pedagogy, but that doesn't mean we can't take planning cues from the children themselves. In my classroom, we have collaborative planning walls which the students can add to at any time.

Planning walls are easy to construct with sugar paper and sticky notes for ideas, but I have also used whiteboard rolls to create a wall where ideas can be adapted and changed if required. I quite like this space to be large so that as many children as possible can participate. There are examples of really creative planning in the primary sector, where teachers are freer from an exam-driven curriculum than their secondary colleagues. I don't think that any of the magic or the excitement is lost if we include the students' ideas in our lessons.

CELEBRATING WORK AND PROGRESS

Aside from planning it is also appropriate to mark progress in your classroom. Not because Ofsted think it is important, but because it helps the children to appreciate what learning they have already done and where they will be going. Classroom spaces should celebrate the efforts and work of the children, and one way to do this is to create something physical in the classroom. This encourages the children to see their learning as a path that has a destination they can all reach.

You could try laminating the titles of the units you have studied on leaves or stars and display them around the door of the classroom. Whenever you reach a learning point as a class, you could join the dots so the children can see their learning journey. This is the classroom wall equivalent of sharing your learning aims with the learners. It is basic good practice to let the children know what they will be studying and their learning goals. This is just one way of letting your classroom space say this for you.

You can also measure progress in your classroom by carefully considering the types of work that you display on the walls. I am a strong advocate of celebrating the children's best efforts, so wall work need not be 'perfect'. In fact, there is nothing more suspicious in a school than a presentation wall of faultless work that shows nothing of the uniqueness or individuality of the children who have made it. What might be worth celebrating for one child is very different to the next, so let your classroom walls honour the individuality of the children you teach and the effort they have made.

When my son was in Year 3 he went for an entire year without having anything he did celebrated – no certificates, nothing mentioned in assembly, no work displayed in the classroom. He is a good kid who tried hard, but he fell short of producing perfect work and so nothing he did ever came up to scratch. The result? A very disengaged child who gave up trying. There is no need to over-praise or be insincere about a child's accomplishments (trust me, they will know if you are not being honest), but we all need encouragement and approval.

One way of being sincere and publically rewarding the behaviours that you want to see more of in your classroom is to award excellent work with a special status. No half measures here: get yourself to Ikea or a car boot sale and buy the biggest and most ridiculously ornate frame you can find. Now spray it gold or something equally eye-catching. If you have a friendly design department you could even ask them to drill some holes in it to add fairy lights. Now, drag the frame into school, batting away the odd looks you get from other staff – they are just jealous of your new find and will soon be wanting one of their own. Next, hang up the frame in your classroom in a prominent place.

Here is the genius bit. If you are working to reward, let's say, resilience, then pick one piece of work that demonstrates resilience and frame it. Get the work up on the wall and show it off to everyone who comes into your room. Make a massive fuss of that piece of work, and make the child feel totally and absolutely epic. The effort you make rewarding positive behaviours will have more impact than punishing negative ones could ever have. So, instead of catching them *out* behaving badly, catch them *in* doing something brilliant, like outstanding homework, and celebrate it. The same technique can be used to commend the use of evaluative language, efforts with handwriting or self-marking.[1]

Another really brilliant idea that I learned from the psychology department at Richard Taunton Sixth Form College is a peer praise board. You need a spare whiteboard for this, but it is totally worth the space. Basically, the class decide at the beginning of the year which characteristics they would like to value as a group. This might include things like:

■ Helpfulness.

■ Always handing in homework on time.

■ Most focused in class.

■ Exceeding their target grade.

■ Most willing to ask relevant questions.

The important point here is that you let the students decide what kind of behaviour they want to reward. Once every half-term you ask the students to vote on who should win each category. You then display the board for the rest of the term, and use every opportunity to big up those students who have been selected. The real value here is that it is the peer group that has chosen what to value, so it is less what the teacher wants and more about what the class recognise as being important. Your classroom can then become a space where you not only do the basic (although very complex) work of teaching, but also where you reinforce the kinds of learners, and adults, you want your class to become.

Learning is not about everybody reaching the top grade. It is about building up and rewarding the type of learning that will, in the long term, make those in your classroom better learners. There is no point teaching classes to parrot facts without them

---

1 For example, using the RAG123 grading system. For more on RAG marking, take a look at Twitter #rag123 for lots of ideas on how educators are using this self-marking and reflection tool.

having the tools they will need to survive on their own later – for example, at university. So, use the wall space in your classroom to help them understand what it takes to be a better learner in life.

VIRTUAL SPACE

As teachers we are often limited by the burdens placed on us in school, and those pressures can stop us from thinking about the bigger picture and what is possible in our lessons. When planning how to teach a subject, how many teachers reach out to experts in those areas? Not many. But speaking to real subject experts can be a key motivator for students.

So, instead of taking them with you in a topic, let the students lead the way by including your students in researching trips or special classroom guests that might be relevant to the learning. It might be hard to get busy people involved in your classroom activities for a day if they have a long way to travel, but more might be willing to Skype or Google Hangout with your class.

CLASSROOM SPACE

How can I have said so much about using the classroom space without discussing furniture layout? A frequently rehearsed debate is whether students should sit in rows facing the teacher, or in small groups to facilitate group work. I think a really good teacher who knows their learners well doesn't mind shifting the furniture about once in a while to suit the needs of the lesson. OK, some teachers swear by having kids sat in rows with the teacher talking at the front. Personally I can think of nothing worse so, for me, groups is the more flexible of the options. But what is important is that what you are doing is working for your class.

Just using the physical space in a different way can cause a stir, but it also refocuses the children on their learning by taking them out of their usual comfort zones. For example, a horseshoe layout can work well for debates and discussions. Or buy some cushions in a charity shop and ask the learners to lie on the floor, using their upturned chairs as a writing desk. Another exciting option is to push the furniture to the sides of the room and get the children to find a space that is comfortable for them.

Learning doesn't have to be a child sitting bright eyed and pen poised at a desk. Learning can also look like children reading standing up against a wall or lying down. It can be quite liberating to see the classroom space being used more naturally by the children. They don't by nature sit at desks – as I'm sure the parent of any child will tell you, they sort of flop about.

In some respects schooling has become a training ground for the stresses of adult life. Yes, of course these children will need to know how to behave appropriately in a job interview, but there is no need for relentless drilling from a very young age. They are children, not mini adults. If your behaviour management is up to scratch, there is a lot of mileage in letting the children be just that – children. I have taught lessons with sitting children under the tables. The important point is that they were still learning, and in the next lesson they were sitting at tables again.

Think about using the space in your classroom as flexibly as you can – not only *how* you use classroom space but also *why*. There is no need to do the things you have always done, and nor is there a need to try every new teaching idea that comes along. But making small changes can have a big impact in terms of engagement and attainment. Use the space, the walls and the furniture differently, or at least think about why you use it in the way you do. It is not habitual practice that makes teaching become entrenched and uninspiring; it is unthinking practice. So, think about your classroom space and consider if you need to make some changes.

> But making small changes can have a big impact

USING SPACE TO ENCOURAGE POSITIVE BEHAVIOURS

Some teachers are lucky enough to have their own classroom – a place they can call their own and in which they have some autonomy. The classroom as a permanent teacher base is more frequent in the primary sector; however, some secondary teachers also have their own rooms. It is much easier to teach in one space from a practical perspective, but it also allows you to use the room to create an ideal teaching environment.

Think about how your room looks as the learners come in. Could you use the space on the door, or around the doorframe, to advertise co-curricular events, or maybe to display some of their work from your lessons? The important point is that you make the learners feel welcome and part of the lesson as soon as they reach the door. The door to your classroom should be special. It marks the transition into your lessons, so it should be different from everyone else's.

Many schools are using research on the positive impact of adults role modelling reading to younger people to encourage their students to read more. You could use your door to inform the students about what book you are reading. (Make sure you are actually reading said book as it would be pretty cringing if a child asked you about it and you did the 'I'm not sure' mini pause before you started talking, which would give you away as a fraud to any small child.) For older readers you could share academic or education books you are reading, as this will demonstrate to them that we can all learn and that you are keen to continue to do so.

I have also used the classroom door as a space to ask learners to share their intentions for the term. I made a big sugar paper tree (harder than you would think) and gave each learner a paper leaf on which they wrote an aim that they would try to achieve that term. This worked really well to focus them at the beginning of the term, but it also made a lovely display of our class intentions that we could then look back on as the weeks progressed.

WHOLE SCHOOL SPACE

Transforming your whole school space can give it renewed purpose. There is a lot you can do to rethink the way the building is used and how it is given meaning. Schools can be a complex hierarchy of centralised power, point scoring and one-upmanship. If your school is like this then you have two choices. The first is to move schools and hope that somewhere else will be different. There is no guarantee of this, so you might be better trying for option two. This involves being an agent for change inside your current school - making a difference for staff and students by transforming it from within.

The biggest shift you can pull off in a school is to make it into an institution that has staff and student buy-in – where mission statements and institutional values actually mean something in the classroom and in the real world. Your school should be a place where everyone feels welcome and able to contribute. Most schools are not run as benign dictatorships, but give staff and students a genuine chance to have their voices and opinions heard. This is a goal to aim towards – and, if you take the time to visit other schools, something you will find you can achieve.

> The biggest shift you can pull off in a school is to make it into an institution that has staff and student buy-in

ASSEMBLIES

There is nothing that unites a whole school like assembly time. Too often, they can be dreary and unenjoyable – delivered by senior teachers about topics of little or no interest to the student body. Even the teaching staff can look bored rigid. You can revamp your assemblies by making them into a space where everyone in the school has an equal right to share what is important to them, and to you all, as a learning community.

The normal teaching staff have given some of the best assemblies I have seen, often about a topic they are interested in or are passionate about. I have recently felt privileged to be in the school body for assemblies about Siberian husky racing in the Arctic, First World War memorials, ultra-running and, perhaps most movingly, a staff member who chose to share her battle with depression. Each one was an insight into the person behind the professional and created real inspiration for the students, as well as forming bonds between the staff as individuals (and not just authority figures) and the student body.

Alongside staff leading assemblies, it is also important for the students to also be involved. Clubs and societies, such as the choir, can use the time to find a vital audience for their work. Other students should also have the opportunity to present assemblies on topics that are of importance to them, and not just sixth-form students or prefects. Again, I have been lucky to be in the audience for student assemblies on the commercialisation of Christmas and a school trip to Africa which had changed the students' perspectives on life. My all-time assembly favourite was when a group of students arranged a singing flash mob. Fabulous. The students and staff left the hall smiling rather than just bored.

A NURTURING SPACE

Students don't just come into school to learn and pass exams. Students come into school to experience life-changing events, to learn skills that will help them when they leave education and, for some, to be nurtured to achieve their potential. This final point may seem obvious, but many learners lack even basic encouragement at home – or on the opposite spectrum they are pressurised by parents. For these students, school can provide a balanced, safe space, full of teachers and activities that build self-confidence, self-awareness and self-esteem.

For some schools, this might involve investing time and energy into projects that can provide these supports to the student body. One example that I have seen run successfully is a cross-school Green Team project. This had a positive impact on the learning environment as it involved the students in an issue much bigger than the school. Of course, this project would be totally different in another school, but at our school it involved a group of staff and students looking to improve the school environment as well as promoting eco-policies and thinking in the school.

Making an impact on the environment is about more than just reducing printing and photocopying, so our Green Team built a low maintenance eco-garden using perennial plants and shrubs that the whole school can enjoy. They also take a lead in ensuring school policies are environmentally friendly. For example, they have made sure that next to every rubbish bin there is a recycling bin, and next to every light switch there is a reminder to turn off lights when the room is not in use.

When I started at the school, one of the things that first caught my eye was this Green Team pledge wall where students across an entire year group had made a pledge to be more environmentally aware.

Now, I know I am biased, but I particularly enjoy seeing collaborative statements like this in a school. I love that the initiative came from the students, and that an idea they had conceptualised made an impact on those at the heart of the school – the students.

Our Green Team also did something that left me totally open-mouthed when I first saw it: they built a kit eco-car and then drove it around the school field. This thing goes up to 30 mph. It certainly felt anarchic seeing a car tear up the playing field – really cool! The kids involved certainly got more out of it than just the experience of building the car. They were able to develop teamwork, leadership and communication skills. This project depended on the generosity of the staff who gave up their free time to help, but the real engine for the idea and making it happen was the students.[2]

A cross-school charities commission has also made my heart sing with the good it has brought out in the students. You would not believe how many doughnuts are sold for charity at my school every term. It is either really inspiring or downright disgusting how many we can eat! The charities group also run all sorts of events by themselves, with little teacher support, because they want to do some good in the world. Fantastic stuff.

LINKING WITH INDUSTRY AND THE WORLD OF WORK

My own role is currently focused on e-learning, so I would recommend that all schools sign up for a British Interactive Media Association (BIMA) Digital Day, or D-Day. BIMA connect schools with those in the digital industries to give students a real flavour of what working in this area might be like. My school was extremely lucky to be partnered with a digital strategy agency, Blue Thirst. There is a significant time investment for the industry professionals involved on the day, but BIMA supplies high quality resources for the teaching staff involved. The sessions are usually designed to run for a whole day, but as we were unable to take a whole class off-timetable, our industry professionals ran lots of small sessions where the activities, such as app design and division of team roles, were completed in an hour.

---

2 Well done to the KES Green Team for all the amazing work they do.

When I started at the school, one of the things that first caught my eye was this **Green Team pledge wall** where students across an entire year group had made a pledge to be more environmentally aware.

GREEN PROMISES

I will compost more often!

I promise to not spend longer than 30 minutes in the shower

recycle waste paper

I'll try not to buy as much STUFF

I promise not to buy any fur coats

I will cycle to school more

I will always turn off lights

I PROMISE TO...
WRITE MY NAME NEATLY ON REVISION BOOKLETS TO SAVE TIPEX.

I will use less CAR

I will remember to always recycle what can be recycled!

I will make sure I don't have unnecessary lights on for example in my horse cage. Thank you.

I will make a compost to he...

The team from Blue Thirst taught every session (and were still smiling by the end of the day!) which was a massive ask. I was particularly impressed by the way they dealt with students from Year 7 to sixth form. They quickly created a positive working relationship and were consistent in checking the students' progress. They encouraged them to think creatively and complete tasks to the best of their ability. Being thrown into a classroom is not everyone's idea of a relaxing break from the office, but as a teacher I am certainly glad that they took the time out from their busy schedules. In particular the digital leaders thrived, and I was very proud of how they rose to the challenge of applying their technical knowledge.

Overall, the day helped to raise the students' awareness of careers in ICT. For a number of students studying ICT and computing is not a priority, but good IT skills would certainly give them an edge in some careers. Another key issue for me was that the learning was contextual and project based so it allowed students to work on their team skills under time constraints, which promoted questioning and debating skills. As a school, we have certainly made a link with industry which otherwise would not have happened had it not been for BIMA. This was as valuable for us as teachers as it was for the students.

In terms of making links that can help your school to thrive, think about using groups that you might already have in school, such as digital leaders, and connecting with other schools who have similar groups. I recently ran a KidsMeet for digital leaders where my school's digital leaders got to make valuable connections with like-minded children from other schools. In-between the student presentations they were put into cross-school, cross-age teams named after tech innovators (such as Lovelace, Jobs, Lane-Fox and Gates). I wanted to encourage them to make links and share knowledge beyond school friendship groups – and I hope this will continue either online or at later events. Once in teams, the students did a carousel of activities run by kind, knowledgeable and expert IT folk. The day was distinguished by this mixture of sharing learning – all of which was given freely, with the children proud to share their accomplishments – and expert tuition. Everyone left buzzing, positive and excited about the learning challenges that lay ahead that term. It reminded me of the exuberant atmosphere that you can get at a TeachMeet. Using the school space to make links with the world outside school can help to focus the children on their current learning and their futures.

So, from your own classroom and how you use it, right up to a whole school approach, there are lots of ways you can rethink and shake up your school to bring benefits to students and staff alike. There is sometimes mileage in doing something that is tried and tested and works, but there is also room in our professional lives to be different, especially when that could have an impact on the lives of our students. Using the space that we have available for learning, and exploiting it to display student work, is something that all teacher geeks should try to do.

TOP GEEK TIPS

- Try to have one activity a term that gives a real world context to the students' learning.
- Embrace assemblies and the opportunities these give you to be a school community.
- If it is not part of your role to see the bigger whole school picture, work with someone who can implement change to make a difference.
- Think of every space in your classroom as a potential learning space.
- Move the furniture – you can always put it back.
- Relinquish the classroom space. Remember, it is your students' classroom.

IN THIS CHAPTER:

- Considering the hows and whys of locating images for use.

- Reconsidering ways in which images can be used, and reused, as part of meaningful teaching and learning.

Chapter 3

READING IMAGES

what do pictures say?

We live and teach in an image saturated world. The media, advertising and the internet have changed forever the way that we view and understand images. But how are images being used in education? Too often, they are a token piece of clip art on a worksheet or a copied-and-pasted image from Google on a PowerPoint. How can we think more meaningfully about images in relationship to classroom practice? The teacher geek uses images in unconventional ways to give students alternative and enhanced learning opportunities.

We live in a world where images are constantly used to engage and manipulate us. Is your classroom a haven of calm and refuge from the visual world? Or is it a place where you recognise that the children bring the world in with them, and if they are used to being stimulated with images then we, as teachers, owe it to them to create an environment that is as stimulating and interesting as the world outside, but with all the learning opportunities possible? For me, our role as teachers should involve making the most of images in our practice, and that means giving some serious thought to how we can use visuals to inspire our students.

LOCATING IMAGES

Of course, we now have the internet to source images. A word of warning, however: it is important to be aware of copyright issues when reproducing images. It is foolhardy to take an image straight from a Google search, particularly as you can find pictures that can be used for non-commercial purposes on websites such as compfight.com. You should also find out about Creative Commons licences. Some images can be used, altered and redistributed, while others are more strictly regulated. Any image that has a 'for use' Creative Commons licence can be used in the classroom.[1]

> **A word of warning:** it is important to be aware of copyright issues when reproducing images.

You can save yourself endless headaches if you name and save images in a logical way. I have a terrible habit of not saving JPEG files with a name that I will be able to find later, and I end up having to trawl through hundreds of pictures to find the one

---

1 For more on Creative Commons licences have a look at Jane Hewitt's *Learning Through a Lens* (Carmarthen: Independent Thinking Press, 2014), pp. 31–33.

I want. My life and yours is too short for that, so come up with a system and stick to it, even if you are pushed for time.

Don't forget to take photographs of any work that your students produce. I quite often tweet pictures of student work in progress and add them to a Pinterest board with ideas from my lessons. This will enable you to share your ideas with the wider world as well as celebrating your students' work in a digital forum (this will be discussed in more detail in Chapter 6). Other teachers have taken ideas from my lessons and improved them, which has been very rewarding and it has improved my teaching practice.

ICONIC IMAGES

So, what kind of images should you be looking for? I would recommend you start with images from contemporary or popular culture, such as album cover art. These are not going to be copyright free, of course, so think hard about how you share them to avoid any potential problems. You can print out in advance album covers either from well-known bands (like the Beatles) or more current artists, and ask students to redesign them around the topic they are studying, focusing on the artwork or the title. The real teaching win here is to get students to think about how the iconic image can be juxtaposed with modern design or techniques. It gets the students' brains firing and thinking about tasks in a different way.

Some really interesting work can be produced by asking students studying feminism, for example, to redesign the artwork for albums by contemporary female artists. Another way that I

have used this technique is to ask students to select images from different album covers to exemplify post-modernist theories. You need a classroom stocked with scissors and glue so that the students can cut and collage during the lesson. You can then use the images they have created as a prompt for a longer piece of writing. This kind of activity enables you to link abstract theories or ideas with something in the real world that students understand. It also helps to develop reasoning and writing around rigorous academic subjects.

CAPTIONING IMAGES

Another way to rethink images is to ask children to describe famous or historical images. I have had great success in doing this when teaching Ancient Greek and Roman history. By taking well-known images and asking children to caption them using contemporary language you can add a level of depth to students' understanding. This technique helps to make historical or formal images more accessible because you are using language with which the students are familiar, but applying it to a formal image that would not normally be described in this way. Mashing up the classical or historical with contemporary language also breaks down the accessibility barriers that can occur with the high culture of art.

You can ask students to describe what the characters featured in an image might be saying or thinking. This allows children to give a voice to the inner lives of individuals and to think about historical events. By giving the children the freedom to bestow language on those represented in the image, they not only become

involved in the creation of a narrative, which reinforces their understanding of the topic being studied, but it also encourages creative thinking around the learning.

A great tool to use in the classroom is Over App, which enables you to add caption text to images. The re-captioned image can then be shared via your VLE or digital space.

IMAGES FROM THE PAST

You can also use images to provide a way in to a new task or topic. For example, if you were studying immigration to the United States you could show the class a photograph of migrants arriving at Ellis Island in the early 1900s. The black-and-white images will add an extra dimension over just reading about it. Why not select a photograph showing lots of people, cut it into sections and give pairs of children different parts of the whole image? Then ask them: what are the people in the image thinking? What kind of conversations might they be having? Then reunite the picture and ask the children to think about what the different parts of the image tell us about the whole. It can be difficult for students to 'read' busy or complex images and find real meaning or insight. By breaking it down into sections, you are giving them an opportunity to access potentially challenging interpretations that might be missed without chunking down the challenge.

You could perhaps start a new topic or area of learning by giving the children images and treating them in a similar way. In this way, they can pursue new lines of enquiry about the learning rather than just being told what they have to study. Images need not dumb down the learning – they can make us ask difficult and uncomfortable questions about ourselves, our learning and the world around us. And how much more intriguing and exciting could it be to be given picture clues about a topic alongside some potential exam questions? Images used carefully alongside demanding questions can help to create challenge and structure thinking processes.

WRITING CHALLENGES USING IMAGES

Images make excellent writing prompts. They are often used with younger children to encourage new or reluctant writers, but there is also a place for visual writing prompts with older writers too. A quick scan of Pinterest will lead to a haul of lots of suitable images. If you have the time and space in your lesson, you could even create your own from drawings, paintings or photographs.

Find an image related to the curriculum or learning you are teaching and ask the children to write a response to it. You could also reuse the same image and ask for a different type of writing – the skills needed to write a report, for example, vary dramatically from those needed to write a letter in character. It can be beneficial to give the children an opportunity to write something that will not be formally assessed, as there is no associated fear of failure. They can just write for the joy of writing, which will have a positive impact on their attitude to learning. Websites such as www.abandoned-places.com can spark the imaginations of older learners and can help to build confidence that will translate into feeling more at ease with writing in general.

www.abandoned-places.com

The children respond to a digital stimulus with 100 words for which they are guaranteed a public forum and helpful feedback. The 100 Word Challenge[2] is a very large project, but you can start small by setting up a class blog and inviting the class next door to leave comments or team up with another school – either way, your children are always working in the knowledge that their work has an audience.

Many schools have word mats available on classrooms desks. The mats include subject-specific vocabulary for children to refer to in order to improve their writing. I would argue that there is a case for including images

100WC.net

you have been using in class to prompt thinking around a topic on the mats. Images can stimulate and promote academic thinking, especially if you have been using them routinely in lessons. They can be a powerful prompt – for example, about the key ideas and themes of a text or topic you are studying. One easy way to make adaptable and high quality looking word mats is to use the iOS app Grafio – you design a template which you can then adapt as the learning moves on over the term.

---

2 See https://100wc.net/.

DIGITAL IMAGES

You can also use augmented reality in the classroom to make images into something more than just a flat visual picture. You can do this using Aurasma, which is an app that allows you to embed video media using an image as a trigger, so when you scan the image the video starts to play. I know this sounds complicated but it is actually very simple.

First you set up an Aurasma channel which others can search for in-app, and follow in a style similar to Twitter. You then need to have both the image you want as the trigger and the video ready on your tablet or smartphone. Once this is done, ask a student to hold a tablet or phone over the image. Aurasma will recognise the trigger image and, as if by magic (and from a really cool purple swirl), the video media will begin to play on top of the image.

Now, the more pressing question is, why might you want to do this? Aurasma enables you to make a display or image interactive, so it has much potential. Here are some ideas:

- Talking posters. Why just have a picture on your wall of Henry VIII when you could have posters that actually feature him talking? The joy of this is that the videos you embed can be made by the students so you will also be celebrating their work.

- Class leaflets or newsletters. Send home documents that embed recordings of sports or drama events. When parents use the app, they will see actual footage.

- Treasure hunt. Create an activity where the students can trigger images which reveal the video clue to the next hidden image.

- You could share best media work with parents by sending home a personalised Aurasma image.

All of these ideas would work well at both primary and secondary level. They make the most of using images and technology to engage learners and parents.

Another great tool is ThingLink, which allows you to embed media content from the internet into a 2D image and make it interactive. The image acts as a trigger in the same way as Aurasma, but instead of the single video appearing, students can embed all kinds of material to make the image interactive. Students can use their own devices to embed media content into an image you have made available on a class account as a summary of their learning beyond the paper resources provided. This image can then be shared with other students by uploading it to the VLE. The images can be an excellent source of revision materials as well as encouraging students to read around a subject area and beyond the set texts. I have often had A level groups reading articles at degree level, and ThingLink certainly helped to encourage them to do this. As they searched for new content to embed in the image, their research inevitably took them to journal articles more advanced than a textbook explanation.

The other brilliant benefit of ThingLink is that it is very flexible and allows learners to express their ideas and research in a variety of ways. For example, students begin their thinking with an image but they are then encouraged to make links to other images, texts and even videos. You can use your completed ThingLink as a starter for the next lesson, or if you set up a class ThingLink page you can set homework where the class have to add a digital resource to a ThingLink image you have created. You could create a ThingLink including all the digital resources needed for a lesson which the students work through at their own pace.

CURATING IMAGES

Another way of using digital images in the classroom is as a visual search engine. Researching and collecting information is an important part of every subject. Whether they are finding out about the Third Reich or researching the importance of narrative in poetry, our learners need to know how to find and store information. In the past they would have done this by looking at books, but lots of us now rely on technology for this visual research. In essence, we are now able to use visual search engines that enable the students to practise two key skills: effective research and understanding how to store information.

There are archives and journals available on the internet, so students need not rely on sites like Wikipedia. But how do they assemble this mass of information? I have found Pinterest really useful for pulling together collections of images. While it is more commonly known for recipes and fashion ideas, there is also a growing educational community using Pinterest as a learning tool.

The best way to use it is to set up a class account. You can then ask the students to use Pinterest as a search engine and research key terms – for example, 'Iliad'. Individual students can then save the 'pins' (images) they find on their own digital boards. The pins store the original URL so the original source can be accessed later. The students can also import pins from other websites, so their research need not be restricted to what is already on Pinterest. There are no lost pieces of paper and students can collaborate by pinning each other's pins.

Despite being a fantastic tool for research, teachers need to keep in mind that Pinterest is a social media platform, so as a teacher you need to be aware that the students can now direct message you with private messages. For the sake of transparency and e-safety, do not engage with them in this way. While this image-driven technology is brilliant and gives the learners opportunities they would not have on paper, you must protect yourself as a professional. This is why a class account that you moderate is the best way of using images on Pinterest.

SOCIAL MEDIA AND SHARING IMAGES

Another excellent image-driven resource that you could use in the classroom is Tumblr. You can use it for assembling textual resources but it is an excellent tool for sharing images. I have found it particularly useful to have a class Tumblr page where students can post images from other websites and use them to inform academic discussions. A class Tumblr page is a really great way of sharing resources and it is a platform that many students will already be comfortable with using.

Tumblr is different from Pinterest because much of the content is from blogs. Tumblr blogs are often very visual which can provide an unintimidating access point which using text alone could not. This can be very useful for starting learning conversations about the current topic being studied. There is nothing quite like a relevant opinion piece to spark a healthy class debate. While I would, of course, love for students to read academic articles, I also appreciate that a wide-ranging reading diet includes opinion pieces, and Tumblr is one way of encouraging children to read more widely. I once had a class where one of the students was so outraged by a piece she read on feminism that she wrote a reply piece. All this came from the simple sharing of images which sparked a desire for her learning to have an impact outside the classroom.

Like Tumblr, a class Instagram account can also provide opportunities for children to share their learning. Again, using social media in the classroom may ring alarm bells for some teachers because of potential e-safety issues. I would argue that the benefits of creating a peer-to-peer sharing environment far outweighs the possible hazards – it is certainly something a well-informed teacher should be able to navigate. Remember, these are platforms for students to upload images of their work to share with other learners, so the focus should be on how they use images for learning.

Unsurprisingly, some older primary aged children have Instagram accounts, so this can be an excellent way of teaching children how social media can be used to share learning and ideas in a responsible way. Making their work public in this way can be a real game-changer for many students who do not make the best effort with their work. Once they see the hard work of others, they are encouraged to do likewise. When I have done this with a class there has been a healthy sense of one-upmanship about the quality of the work being shared, and it has raised the overall quality of the work being produced. I don't know about you, but I am willing to give anything a go that raises attainment in my classroom. Teachers might not feel comfortable with using this kind of approach, but I would definitely encourage you to give it a try.

I hate the phrase '21st century classroom' to describe the use of innovative technology. We have been in the 21st century for over a decade, so we should stop thinking of ourselves as pioneers of the new, but rather as exploiting technologies that are in many ways ephemeral. The digital platforms and technologies we use to access learning will no doubt continue to change; however, the significance and usefulness of the visual image in the classroom is perpetual. Images are part of our shared values and culture so we should be using them to give learning an added dimension. A geek teacher will look to exploit all potential learning opportunities, and be comfortable with taking risks by working with resources from outside their subject area.

TOP GEEK TIPS

- Get parents involved in the learning in your classroom by posting student work using social media so they can see their children's learning.

- By using images, the work your students produce will be visually striking. Put it up on the walls for all to see.

- Set up a class Tumblr or Instagram account, and take the learning to the digital spaces the children already inhabit.

IN THIS CHAPTER:

- The impact of sound and music on learning.
- The importance of music in the whole school context.

Chapter 4

SOUND WAVES

retune your ears

I can just about deal with the idea of a classroom that is silent occasionally, but one that is quiet for the majority of time fills me with a sense of foreboding. Children naturally make lots of noise, but that doesn't mean that they are necessarily distracted or not learning. Of course, there are times when silence is appropriate - you would be a poor teacher if you sent students to take exams without first doing some mocks - but fundamental to transforming your classroom is thinking about sound and how it can be used to motivate students and help them learn. A geek teacher is happy with using sound to redefine how we learn in the classroom, as well as celebrating the power that music can have on individuals and groups of students.

WELCOMING CHILDREN TO YOUR CLASSROOM

Over the last few years I have started every lesson by playing some music. A whole variety of music – from The Clash to Taylor Swift to Beethoven. I organise the beginning of my lessons so that students know what to expect, and the routine helps them to settle down and start their learning quickly with the minimum of fuss.

I select a song from YouTube to welcome them to the classroom and to define the transition from one subject to another. They have often never heard what I am playing them before, and they respond in a variety of ways from ignoring it to dancing into the room. (I had one class with a lot of performing arts students who delighted in the music and would bust some pretty impressive moves!)

The point of the music at the beginning of the lesson is not just to wake them up; the point is to train them to be in the room (i.e. punctual) and to be working on the starter activity before the end of the song. In schools where behaviour is not a major issue, the punctuality and learning readiness of the children can be taken for granted. However, creating positive patterns of behaviour, so that children understand what is expected from them and are willing to participate in the lesson from the outset, is undeniably valuable. The music signals to the children what they need to do, without me cajoling them. This leaves me free to greet them by the classroom door, make sure everyone is welcomed and talk to every single student on his or her way into the lesson. Some children can go for a whole school day without being asked how they are, or being spoken to in a friendly way. Don't be that teacher.

The metronome scale markings (left column top to bottom): 40, 44, 48, 52, 56, 60, 66, 72, 80, 88, 96, 104, 112, 120, 132, 144, 160, 176, 192, 208

The metronome scale markings (right column top to bottom): 42, 46, 50, 54, 58, 63, 69, 76, 84, 92, 100, 108, 116, 126, 138, 152, 168, 184, 200

Tempo markings (centre): Largo 40–60, Larghetto 60–66, Adagio 66–76, Andante 76–108, Moderato 108–120, Allegro 120–168, Presto 168–208

PACING ACTIVITIES

Sound can be very useful when you need to change the pace of activity in a classroom. If you have a quick-fire activity, such as writing an answer on a mini whiteboard, playing the *Countdown* music can encourage the children to finish promptly. If you are doing a whole class task for a set period of time, the activity can be nicely framed using music. It could be classical music or pop music – whatever feels right for the class at that time – so go with your instinct.[1]

1 I will state at this point there is never a good reason for playing 'Gangnam Style' – unless you really want to see the whole of a Year 9 class do *that* dance move.

For example, I have a giant Jenga set on which I write questions for the learners. They have to pull out a block and answer the question on it. Now, this works perfectly well as a task on its own, but it is super-charged by playing what I call 'epic music', which heightens the sense of anticipation and drama in the room. Seriously, 'epic music' is an actual thing – go and search for it on YouTube.

YouTube is often blocked by the firewall filters in some schools. If this is the case in your school, I assume you have already done the logical thing and asked for it to be unfiltered and someone (probably not a teacher) has refused. If that is the case you could always try seeking out music to use on an alternative such as Vimeo or ZippCast. Alternatively, if you have music stored on your phone, you could always plug that into the speakers or use the 3G on your smartphone to connect to YouTube which won't be affected by filtering.

CREATING AN AURAL CLASSROOM ATMOSPHERE

Another way to think about using music is to set the tone for a lesson. From spooky music to accompany writing about Bram Stoker, to using film soundtracks to create tension while discussing dramatic techniques, the music can set the feel of the lesson and provide a hook to draw in learners.

It can sometimes be really hard for students to make the cultural links between ideas and some areas of knowledge, so providing a sound-based framework can offer a way in for them. When studying other cultures, historical events or anything that has a distinct cultural otherness, the shared experience of listening to music can provide a way to access the learning. For the centenary of the First World War, for example, some schools had class activities and assemblies to commemorate an event which can be very difficult for children to comprehend. Playing music from the period can give children an opening to think about the loss of life in the conflict. They may not be able to understand the mechanised killing of millions of people, but they can understand the emotion conveyed in music written around the time – for example, Elgar's 'Nimrod'. You could also play them some of the songs designed to encourage men to enlist, like 'Pack Up Your Troubles', as an avenue for thinking about why people went to fight.

Often, what attracts children to learning about a subject is that they see it as being interesting or strange. In my own classroom, the otherness of Ancient Greek culture, for example, attracts them to the topic. In no other lesson would they learn why sheep had water poured over their heads prior to ritual sacrifice.[2] The information in itself may be fascinating, but you can further heighten their curiosity by playing a piece which embodies music from the period. (Historians out there: before you tell me off that any musical re-creation might not be accurate, please remember that this is about sparking curiosity in the learners by making the topic less two-dimensional.)

LINKING SOUND AND IMAGES

Music can be used to encourage students to think critically about filmic source material. Try playing your students a key clip from a film that you would normally use to enhance their understanding of a topic, but then ask them what alternative background music could be used and how it would change the mood and meaning of the film. This kind of activity requires sophisticated analysis skills, and can stimulate students into developing their extended writing abilities and therefore improve their attainment.

Alternatively, play a clip without sound and then discuss how music might add to the atmosphere of the scene. This works especially well with thrillers. You could develop this task by asking the students to choose or create a soundtrack to accompany their written work. If they have devices such as iPads, there is also a lot of teaching mileage in asking children to make videos using apps such as Explain Everything to

---

2 It was so they appeared to nod and was interpreted as them agreeing to the sacrifice, which was a good omen. Really.

support their learning. Music can be a crucial part of this, especially if part of the process involves the students reflecting on why they made certain choices and what effect they hoped they would have on the viewer.

SPARKING CURIOSITY ABOUT OTHER CULTURES

If you are studying a geographically (rather than historically) distant culture, you can spark interest in the classroom by listening to music from that region, or maybe several different types of music that show the diversity of other cultures. It would be pretty naff to introduce a culture with potentially stereotypical music – but this only goes to show that, when thinking about the complexities of a society, music can be an excellent way in. For example, my son has studied Japan at primary school, as part of which he was played traditional Japanese music as well as more contemporary pop. This gave him, at quite a young age, an accessible way to think about Japanese culture.

When teaching the notion of British identity to an AS sociology class, I used a similar approach to encourage the students to think about what Britishness might mean. I asked them to create a playlist of music that represented Britishness. What a mix I got back! Everything from hymns they had sung at primary school, to classical music, to the Beatles and Dizzee Rascal. Thinking about the music that represented their own culture gave the students an inroad to thinking meaningfully about the difficulty of defining identity in a post-modern multicultural world. Interesting stuff, indeed, for my second ever lesson with them. It also gave them the opportunity to think about a subject before they had acquired the technical language they thought they would need for such a discussion to take place.

THE POWER OF THE SPOKEN WORD

BBC Radio Four recently produced a brilliant programme analysing the effects of ethnicity and class on educational attainment, which featured the work of Tony Sewell. It was gold dust for my AS sociologists, so I ripped it from iPlayer to use in the lesson. I wanted the students to listen, *really listen*, and not to take notes or be distracted, so I asked them to close the blinds. We then turned off the lights and they lay on the floor - as did their slightly overenthusiastic teacher! The effect of the dark initially disconcerted them, but they soon settled and I had their total concentration for the half-hour radio programme. Obviously, it was a novelty to interact with the classroom space in a different way. However, I felt the real win was the depth of the discussion which followed. They had really listened to the content of the programme - in reality, they'd had very little choice. It was a kind of sensory deprivation. But because they only had the audio stimulus, they were able to use the time in the darkened space of the classroom to thoroughly process and think about the information they were being given, and make connections to previous learning.

I have discovered that audio alone can be very powerful. We assume, as teachers, that we need to engage the students using the digital media that is all around them. However, our learners can also be captivated by simple techniques and being asked to learn in new ways. Just like some teachers might be wary of using technology, I guess some might also be wary of giving students opportunities like this. It requires a mutual relationship of trust. The students must trust you that there is value in what you are asking them to do, and it is worth their time to try something new. In turn, you must trust them to respond with maturity to a new environment and a different type of task.

I have started to use this technique a lot when teaching the *Iliad*. I have found that listening to the book read aloud (as opposed to reading them aloud ourselves) in a darkened room intensifies the way students imagine and visualise the events in the story. I obviously can't see what is going on inside the students' heads, but the writing they have produced following these auditory sessions has been of a very high quality with lots of attention to detail. It might be the aural experience, or it might be simply giving them some time and space in the day to be still and really focus. But this experience has certainly done something to improve their written work – and that is a win that I will take away.

SPECIAL EDUCATIONAL NEEDS AND DISABILITY LEARNERS

Many students use music and sound in their lives – it is rare to see a teenager on a bus without headphones on. Music is powerful and can be used to convey emotion and meaning. For some young people, sound is ever present in their lives to the extent that silence can be actually uncomfortable. There are also children with special educational needs and disability (SEND) needs who find silence difficult or distressing.

As a teacher, it is important to create a classroom climate that welcomes all and allows everyone to work to the best of their ability. During activities that require quiet time, try playing some unobtrusive white noise to see if that helps your learners to focus. You can experiment with what kind of sounds might work by browsing audio files on soundbible.com. As a solution for longer periods of time, consider finding a suitable audio file on YouTube and putting it through an infinite looper-style website so that you don't have to keep pressing play. I have found that students are really happy to work with background noise, and for a number of them it can make a real difference to their ability to focus.

USING TECHNOLOGY TO CREATE SOUND AND MUSIC

There are a number of possibilities for students to create their own sounds and music. During my technology and creativity lessons, when the children are off-timetable, I use various apps (e.g. GarageBand, Spreaker) to teach children key skills – such as teamwork, leadership, being proactive and taking responsibility for their own work – that they will need later in life. They can use the app to write their own track, which is valuable as it is an opportunity they might not have had previously, especially in a classroom environment where they can bounce ideas off each other and get peer feedback. The really exciting part, however, is when they collaborate in small groups to create a track. This gives them the opportunity to work on perfecting a piece of work they can be really proud of, but also, crucially, to refine their negotiation skills. It is a total pleasure seeing them produce something together from scratch, but even more impressive is the way they work together to agree on the creative direction of the project – something that many adults would struggle with!

In fact, creating a piece of music can help us to commit information to memory. A quick search of YouTube will show you just how many students either rewrite song lyrics or create new pieces to help them remember academic content. I can't recite the alphabet without merging into the version that is set to 'Twinkle Twinkle Little Star' (the reason, I reckon, that some children get confused around the LMNOP section!), so creating a revision song can be a fantastic way to remember key knowledge. They can listen to it on their phone on the way to and from school. This rewriting technique works really well with very familiar lyrics, so perhaps try some Disney songs – there is nothing like a bit of classroom cartoon nostalgia to get the creative juices flowing!

USING SOUND AS PART OF MANAGING YOUR CLASSROOM

Sound can be used in your classroom as part of a behaviour management strategy. In my first and second year classes, I use a call-and-response clapping signal to attract students' attention. It gets their attention without me having to raise my voice, plus they like to feel part of a group action. The power of feeling part of something bigger than yourself is one of the gifts that music and sound can give your class.

If your students come in after lunch break in a very boisterous mood, try playing them a calming choral or classical piece and they will start to settle down. Do they need some motivating in that last lesson on a Friday? Nothing cheers up a tired class like some Bob Marley. And you can't imagine how happy my Year 7 class are when, at the end of a really tough lesson, I play them the internet classic 'Pink Fluffy Unicorns Dancing on Rainbows'!

MUSIC BRINGS US TOGETHER

Music can bring a whole school together, transforming the way that children feel not only about their learning but also about themselves. Generations of children have sung together in assemblies, but you can take school unity to a whole new level by asking the children to write a school song that embodies the values of the institution. This is especially suited to younger children who can feel genuine pride in being involved in such a project. It can be performed for the whole school and taught to other classes. We have a national anthem, so why not a school anthem too!

Think about how you use music and sound in your classroom and your school, and do not underestimate how crucial they can be when it comes to motivating, engaging and hooking in learners. Geek teachers know when silence is appropriate, but they also know how to use sound and music to bring the learning in their classrooms alive.

TOP GEEK TIPS

- Play music at the beginning of every lesson to set the tone for the lesson and to welcome the children.

- Use music or sound discretely from other resources to hook in the learners.

- Let the children make their own music to boost their learning.

IN THIS CHAPTER:

- Stocking your classroom for students to make and learn.

- Improving student thinking skills with non-traditional teaching objects.

Chapter 5
MEND AND MAKE
(or why you always need plastic cups, tinfoil and marshmallows in your classroom)

Have you ever stood in front of a class of children who just did not understand what you were trying to explain to them? Of course you have. You, me and every other teacher in the land. So what do you do? Try to explain it again? Explain it a different way? Point to the writing on the board? Try to explain it individually? Ask their peers to explain? Every teacher in the country has had a starring role in the 'explain pantomime', alongside a supporting cast of classmates and teaching assistants.

But what is really happening here? Individual children who do not understand will end up feeling isolated, exasperated and disconnected from the learning – not just in your lesson but also with school in general – so it is vital that we address the problem. Geek teachers are happy to try something new to engage disaffected learners, and that should include creative hands-on activities.

BEWARE THE
SELF-FULFILLING PROPHECY

Back in 1992, my presumably well-meaning maths teacher told me not to worry about the 'hard questions' because I was 'never going to be any good at maths'. At that moment I gave up on trying at maths. I was put in the bottom set and lived up to the self-fulfilling prophecy: I never did well in maths. Teachers came and went, and we all just about scraped through. To this day, when presented with numbers my brain turns itself off – maths is not for the likes of me. I wonder now how different my experience of maths might have been if we had been taught in a different way.

It's not just maths. For me, maths was the subject that made school really unpleasant, but for other learners it can be English or languages. Any subject can cause the blank disassociated look of a learner who has switched off. In terms of subjects I have taught, this happens most often when I am trying to explain theoretical perspectives. I find theory very interesting, and in my first few years of teaching sociology I assumed everyone else would too. So off I went, covering the whole board in Hegelian dialectics and happily spouting on about historical materialism. I turned around and was faced with a sea of tilted heads (a sure sign that learners don't understand) and blank faces. Then it dawned on me: I can't teach like this. It might make sense to me, but no one else in the room has the foggiest what the teacher is going on about. So, over the following years I worked really hard to teach differently.

(or why you always need plastic cups, tinfoil and marshmallows in your classroom)

WHY MAKE IN YOUR CLASSROOM?

Consider Bloom's taxonomy. There are, of course, problems with thinking about learning as being hierarchical. However, I find the concept of a pyramid structure quite helpful, especially if you consider that 'create' is at the top. Think about your own lessons. How often are children given the chance to create something? Obviously, writing and crafting written work is a form of creativity – this is something I will consider in more depth in Chapter 7.

For now, I would like to think about making physical objects to help students understand difficult or complicated concepts. There is pleasure and joy in seeing children of all ages create something. This need not be, and should not be, confined to younger children or the art classroom. Lots of primary schools up and down the country have creative curriculums that allow children to do rather than just see. Why look at a worksheet about meanders when you can model one? Why try to teach about neutrons without recreating their action in the playground?

Primary practitioners understand the power of making and modelling to absorb the learner and to provoke associations with other areas of knowledge. This is something very positive that teachers can take into the secondary classroom. Don't worry about mess – you can tidy it up. Don't worry about what teachers are doing in the classrooms next door. There is a good chance it isn't what you are doing, but quite frankly, who cares? You cannot imagine the chaos in my classroom that led to these wonderful 3D models of sociological theories (see pages 80–81). The mess was so worth it!

STOCKING YOUR CLASSROOM

I will outline some ideas for making in your
classroom. But first you are going to have to be
open-minded about every child working on something
different. It has taken me years as a teacher to
move past the point of thinking that they should
all be working on the same task, and that their
learning should all look the same, in process and
product. It doesn't and we shouldn't force it.

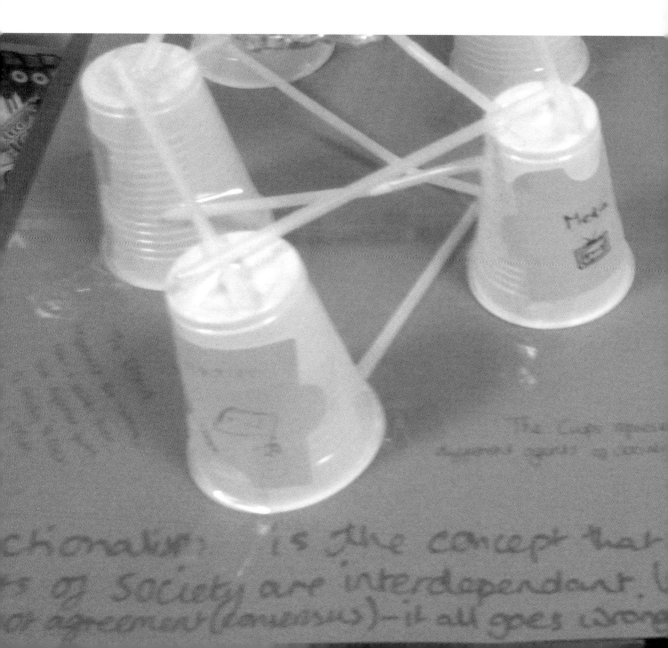

(or why you always need plastic cups, tinfoil and marshmallows in your classroom)

Treat your classroom like Jamie Oliver thinks you should treat your kitchen store cupboards. Always have a stock of things available to help children create. For me the list would include:

- Packets of straws.
- Plastic cups.
- BBQ kebab sticks (feel free to blunt them).
- Tinfoil.
- Modelling clay.

You may also need an occasional stock of marshmallows …

EDIBLE MAKING

Edible making is my favourite activity. Often in lessons we are exploring relationships or connections between people, characters or the causes of an event. So, for example, when teaching a complex piece of poetry, I ask my students to model the links between the characters using marshmallows. They write the names of the characters on the marshmallows (use edible baking pens) and then use BBQ sticks to create the connections. You can even go a stage further and ask the students to attach sticky notes to the sticks explaining the relationships between the characters.

This sort of activity can help students to understand quite complicated connections which otherwise might have been difficult to visualise. It also creates a very striking piece of 3D sculpture. I would advise you to take photographs of the work (it won't last long!). The students can then use the images to inspire longer pieces of writing about the text. Using a prompt that they have made themselves for extended pieces of writing is a good way to reinforce information that you need students to remember over the long term. They encounter the information various times: when making the object, when thinking about connections and again when crafting a longer piece of writing. This serves to reinforce the connections between key facts. And as an added bonus, you can let the students munch the marshmallows afterwards, which dramatically cuts down on the tidying up!

(or why you always need plastic cups, tinfoil and marshmallows in your classroom)

JUNK MODELLING

I once had to teach a class of students about theoretical approaches to social inequality from 1950 to the present day. This was about as interesting to them as watching paint dry. In fact, if I had asked them if they would rather watch paint dry the answer would have been yes. So, in a moment of off-piste teaching (the sort that isn't on a lesson plan – because, let's face it, they are a rough guide and not a diktat), I decided to get a load of cardboard boxes of different sizes (which is why you need to be on good terms with the premises staff and reprographics team) and used them to create a 3D sculpture that represented the relative importance of various theories according to the class (as in the picture on page 84).

The Marxism box was huge and the post-modernism box was an ironic paper plate. Once the boxes had been assembled, the students annotated and decorated them with the concepts behind the theories. Yes, I let them have glitter too. The whole creation lived at the side of my classroom for the entire term and was part of the landscape that they looked at when they should have been doing something else. However, it transpired that by having the boxes in the room, the class managed to absorb the shapes that they made. As a result, they could write a convincing account of theoretical approaches to social inequality by visualising the boxes and then applying their knowledge of the theories. It essentially became an aide-memoire to help them visualise their learning as a shape rather than just content.

I think that this type of teaching approach – where the students make first and then use what they have made to help them frame their knowledge – is quite brave. I admit that I didn't know what the end result would be when the students first started using the boxes. This was not purely reckless of me. I had an idea that it would work, and as a stand-alone lesson and

(or why you always need plastic cups, tinfoil and marshmallows in your classroom)

introduction to the topic it certainly did work. It was serendipity that gave it the long-term impact on the students that it did.

This is pretty exemplary of how some of my best ever lessons have happened. I have something totally predictable planned, but I let myself be brave enough to wonder, 'What might happen if …?' I was daring enough to try something different, and to let the learning take place in a less formally structured way – and it still had impact on their understanding of the topic. It is OK to try out novel approaches in lessons – if you didn't you would be the exact same teacher who stumbled out of teacher training all those years ago. In so many ways, not refining and adapting your practice is a waste of experience and the opportunity to improve.

THE POWER OF MAKING

Remember at the beginning of this chapter I suggested that you should have a fully stocked classroom? This is why: in those not-on-the-lesson-plan moments, it is much easier for you to bust out and try something new if you have the materials on hand to do so. If all you have is paper then you are limited to using just that. Before you get cross with me and tell me that there is lots you can do with paper, I do know this – I promise.

However, what I want to explore here are the rich possibilities for spontaneous making. Not the sort of pre-planning demanded by papier mâché, but the kind of ad-hoc making that might help to illustrate or explain a key concept or idea (for example, I have used this technique with AS classes to model difficult concepts at the beginning of the course). This is where your pound shop stash of tinfoil, paper cups and straws can really come into its own. So, imagine you are a student (stop looking at the clock!) and you have been in a lesson about functionalism for 30 minutes (your problem for choosing sociology A level). Once you have done the reading, please can you make me a model of what functionalism looks like? You have 10 minutes … Go!

Much more thought goes into thinking what functionalism is all about in those 10 minutes than if you had asked students to fill in a worksheet. They are also able to work together to model something quite unique. It is worth commenting that if your students spend time and effort making something, then you shouldn't just bin it at the end of the lesson. This might mean you have a classroom full of strange creations, but it doesn't hurt to keep them for a few weeks to model understanding. In fact, they can be a useful tool to demonstrate to students how their understanding has progressed and become more sophisticated. This opportunity for reflection on students' learning is a valuable one – in this case, modelled powerfully by the presence of a handmade object.

MAKING TO DEVELOP ESSAY WRITING

Searching out opportunities to add depth and understanding to student knowledge can go hand in hand with developing skills such as essay writing. Much of what is required of students, particularly in exams, is to retain in-depth knowledge that has little application to their real lives, yet will have a very real factor in determining what their lives will be like in terms of exam attainment.

Students tend to respond well to a task if it asks them to develop exam skills, and thus revise content knowledge. By 'respond' I mean to engage, complete and work to the best of their abilities. I might even throw in enjoying the learning and accepting that some things are hard and take time to master. This is not a classroom culture that just appears overnight; you need to work hard to create it. The brightest kids in the world can still give up trying if they don't understand the value of the struggle and how to overcome it.

With this in mind, I developed an activity that would encourage the students to make evaluative links between two sets of information. The students had already read the primary texts, which in this case was the *Iliad*, and had done the required classroom work, so we had a lesson free to try something new. In advance of the lesson, I created a sheet of prompts, some of which were images and some were key quotes from the text. The images included a mixture of pop/contemporary visuals and more traditional images, plus some diagrams. I asked the students to create an annotated collage that used the images to deconstruct the work (and their accumulated understanding) of the main ideas they had learned so far in this area. They began by cutting out pictures and then creating links to show how the images related to each other. This might sound easy but, of course, there is no one 'right' answer – just different opinions about what theories link certain concepts to other ideas, or provide a critical evaluation of those ideas.

Much of the joy in this type of work comes from giving the learners an open-ended task. You would be surprised how many of them find this type of activity difficult simply because they are not used to it. Remember, difficult is not something you avoid as a teacher. Difficult is what work should be. No one gains anything at all from kids tearing though easy work which presents no real challenge for them. So, be happy as a teacher to give your students work which they find challenging or activities that stretch them to work or think in a way that is unfamiliar.

Once the learners had decided on the arrangement of the images, I encouraged them to stick them down and then annotate them with the links they had identified. It can be very interesting to see what learners come up with – they often make links that you had not thought of as being the most obvious ones. It can also be revealing of the students' depth of knowledge and understanding – the quality of their annotation will expose the level they have reached. For example, a student with less knowledge might be able to label an idea as Marxist, while a more well-informed student might know which theorist made a particular comment or be able to attribute a specific idea to a writer. Students with really good recall will also be able to tell you the relevant year and be able to make evaluative links with oppositional thinkers. You could, of course, ascertain all this information from other forms of assessment. However, it is worth remembering that the element of the unusual draws in children. Mocksteds and practice writing have their place in the classroom, but there should also be a place for making and using the outcomes to prompt deeper enquiry into a subject area.

MODELLING CLAY

Your classroom store cupboard should never ever be without modelling clay, although the best kind is the dough you can make yourself from flour, water and salt. This is actually quite fun - plus you can add glitter, which will rub off on the students so they look like a David Bowie tribute act, which is funny in itself. That aside, you can do some really interesting things with modelling clay - I have seen it used in geography lessons to model the structure of the earth's crust using different coloured layers.

You can ask the children to fashion just about anything from modelling clay. Here are some ideas:

- How they feel about a particular topic.
- An alternative ending to a play or text.
- A model to demonstrate their learning that lesson as a plenary activity.
- To represent the view of a particular theorist or writer.
- A model that reflects their behaviour in the lesson.
- A model reflecting an aspect of their learning – and a partner has to guess what it represents (my all-time favourite).

The possibilities are endless and can be easily adapted for any age and any classroom. If I might make one small suggestion, it would be to have some wet wipes handy in case the tables get covered in goo – it seems to dry harder than concrete.

Teaching in a classroom where you are prepared to let learners experience their learning in novel ways can add an extra dimension to their understanding. It's not that kids can't learn without a little fun, and nor is it this is fun, meaningless and purposeless. It's about giving over time and space to do something different that may well have massive impact in terms of information retained which can then be called on under exam conditions. Try it: be a geek teacher and rethink the ways that you let students demonstrate their progress and their learning.

(or why you always need plastic cups, tinfoil and marshmallows in your classroom)

TOP GEEK TIPS

- It's OK to go off-lesson plan and do some making if it is appropriate to the learning.

- Keep your classroom store cupboards well-stocked.

- Let children make using different mediums. It's great to encourage individual expression.

IN THIS CHAPTER:

- The arguments for and against sharing student learning.

- How to share work with e-safety in mind.

- Why sharing work celebrates learning.

Chapter 6

SHARING LEARNING

life is too short for worksheets

When I went to school in the 1980s and 1990s our work was never shared with parents or peers. Occasionally a grainy photocopy might go home in a newsletter to parents or some pieces of exemplary artwork might be displayed on the wall, but I've got to be honest that my work was never perfect enough to be considered for parental or public display. Multiply that by every classroom in my school, and every school in my town, and every town in the country, and that is a lot of children working hard for no one but the teacher to see their work.

It is now one of my core beliefs that the work of every child should be celebrated, seen and shared. Not just with parents but with a wider audience. A geek teacher should relish the opportunities that sharing student work can bring.

WHY MIGHT YOU NOT WANT TO SHARE YOUR STUDENTS' WORK?

Before I explain why (and how) we should share teaching and learning, it seems pertinent to consider the objections to sharing students' work online. The first argument put forward is that sharing work online encourages or aids cheating. You know the scenario: you set work and the first thing a child does is to google the title. In theory they could then copy and paste the answer, but I would assume (and I don't think this is too optimistic) that this wouldn't happen because you have taught them the importance of valuing their own work. Furthermore, students can be dissuaded from doing this because they know that you know them quite well, and so would be familiar with their writing style and capabilities. If you were to set an essay on Marxism, and a student handed in a piece making reference to Hegelian dialectics, when previously they had struggled to understand the term 'capitalism', then it doesn't take a rocket scientist to know foul play is afoot. It never hurts to point this out to the children.

The second reason is that some teachers, and more often parents, have concerns about their child's work being read online. The conversation might go like this:

Concerned parent: But what if someone sees the essay that William has written?

Me (beaming): Yes, they probably will. Isn't it brilliant?!

What is happening here is a misunderstanding of what the internet can offer the children in our classrooms as academic learners. The parent is (rightly) concerned that their child could be exposed to cruel feedback from peers or trolls. The online essay appears to be an e-safety issue. These fears are compounded by the concern that children might give away personal information, and even be traceable via shared online work. Personally, I think this is an example of the kind of moral panic that is fuelled by those who do not use the internet much and have not seen the great work that schools are doing to make children more savvy about online threats and their digital footprint.

HOW CAN YOU SHARE LEARNING SAFELY?

As a teacher you can take several steps to ensure that the children whose work you are sharing are safe. First, make sure you are sharing the work with the blessing of the senior leadership team (SLT) – they will probably have policies in place to help you do so safely. There might already be a teacher in your school who is tech savvy and can help to guide you. If this is not the case, then congratulations, you are a trailblazer. How exciting! Work with the SLT to create policies that will shape the future of your school. You might like to think of your sharing as a trial. I find that calling this 'educational research', which it is (at a push), often helps to encourage people to help and support you with using technology in the classroom to make learning more purposeful.

Second, you need to address parents' quite legitimate anxieties. Of course parents worry about their children: they want them to have the best possible education. To that end, it never hurts to write home and explain what you are doing and why. Let parents know where they can find work from other schools online so that you have a positive review audience ready to go.

The most undesirable situation is that they find out via their children what has been happening and don't understand your intentions. Imagine the situation. You know how pooped children are at the end of the school day – all they want to do is go home, eat snacks and flop about on the sofa. (My own boys

only communicate in grunts until they have been fed dinner.)
So, this conversation might ensue:

Lovely interested parent: What did you do at
school today?

Teenager: (Grunt) Nothing.

Lovely interested parent: Well, you must have
done something for six hours?

Teenager: We put our work on the internet for
other people to criticise.

This would set alarm bells ringing for even the most enlightened
parent, so don't let it arise. Get the parents involved and
on-board from the start, whether you are setting up a class blog
at the beginning of the year where digital work can be displayed,
or whether your school is introducing a parent password section
to the VLE. The last thing you need is a parent ringing your
head teacher, or Ofsted, because they think you are putting
their child in danger.

Do whatever you need to do to create the confidence that what
you are doing is safe and supported by your school, and that
sharing will benefit your learners. As well as getting the backing
of your SLT, you might also want to discuss your plans with
your local child protection team or e-safety officer, if you have
one. Make sure that the advice that you get is from someone
reputable and knowledgeable, and that you implement it in a
way that is in line with your school policies. There are several
really excellent national organisations that can also provide

guidance, such as Childnet and the South West Grid for Learning.

In some cases, I advocate pushing at educational boundaries, but this is one example where you are best playing it safe in order to build positive relationships with parents and be a good role model for other staff. One parental complaint about using the internet to showcase work can put the kibosh on future projects for years to come, so work with the fearful to show them the benefits. All that being said, do not be afraid of making students' work available online.

HOW CAN YOU SHARE THE LEARNING WITH THOSE OUTSIDE YOUR CLASSROOM?

So, you have done your research, spoken to the right people and feel relatively confident about using the internet as a platform to make your students' work public. What else should you consider? One concern which frightens a lot of staff is that the technology might not work – the computers might not log on, the internet has a funny five minutes or the awesome website you wanted to use no longer exists. As the teacher, you can take some sensible precautions to try to

ensure that the lesson doesn't tank, but part of
using IT in your lessons is accepting that there
might be a few hiccups.

You can think about this in two ways. The first is a 'Well, bugger me, I won't use it at all' attitude. However, given the range of opportunities the web offers for making students' work public, I think this is the least satisfactory. Your students will certainly be using digital technologies as they grow older – it will be an element of the vast majority of jobs when they enter the workforce. By denying them the opportunity to learn digital skills you are in fact short-changing them. I know it can be tempting to assume they will learn everything they need to know in dedicated ICT lessons, but the weight of making our children safe and savvy about how to use the internet lies with all education professionals. It is a whole school effort.

The second response to recognising that the IT might not always work as intended is to always have a plan B to meet the objectives of the lesson, regardless of computer/website/ internet failure. A good back-up plan should always be part of your lesson planning – it will save you when the panic starts to kick in.

IT PRECAUTIONS

As well as having a plan B, there are a number of
precautions you can take to ensure the lesson runs
as smoothly as possible. Here are my suggestions:

■ Make sure that the computers are working properly the day before.

■ Check any additional equipment such as microphones and headphones.

■ Make sure you are running a web browser that will support the activity you have planned.

■ Check that the children have log-ins and passwords that work. (Getting them to remember said passwords is another kettle of fish all together. Some schools make little credit card sized reminders, but I advocate each child having a word they always use, and then add to it the first four letters of the website they are using – for example, to log in to Google they might have GOOGUSUALWORD and perhaps add their year of birth at the end.)

■ Ask the children to log in as soon as they enter the room and while you are explaining the task. This cuts down on time lost waiting for computers to start up. It is handy to set the task online too so that they can refer to the lesson aims as their work progresses.

■ Know the phone extension of your IT support team. These individuals are indispensable to you, so treat them like royalty (or at least buy them some biscuits every so often and always say thank you).

■ Check the website the night before to confirm that it still exists and appears to be working.

■ Trial the activity you have set on a student computer to make sure that it can be completed.

■ Decide on a way of collecting in the students' work once they have completed it. You can ask them to email it to you, but this may just clog up your inbox and provide very few meaningful opportunities for feedback. I would advise you to collect in work digitally via a platform such as Google Classroom, which also enables you to provide good quality feedback. Do not fall into the trap of asking children to print out work they have produced digitally to stick in their books. Not only does it cost a fortune in printing, but it also wastes the opportunity to provide digital feedback. If you really need to see work in their book, then ask them to produce it there in the first place. If not, then work out a way of signalling where the digital feedback can be found. Some schools use stickers or stamps in the children's books that indicate that digital comments can be found on Google Drive, the school network or VLE.

If you take these precautions then your digital lessons will run a lot smoother. I know it looks like a long list, but as you embed the use of technology in more of your lessons, much of the checking will become second nature.

BLOGGING

Even more important than what we can achieve as teachers is what the children can achieve as learners. Giving your students a real voice that can be heard outside the classroom is the best way to accomplish this. So, share their successes and their learning adventure by setting up a class blog. Nothing in the world encourages the good practice of proofreading and revising written work than knowing that the head teacher, parents and, in fact, anyone in the world can read what you have done. I have seen children who had previously written very little contribute many pages of well-considered work, and I have others who often write over-lengthy pieces think meaningfully about how to convey their meaning more concisely.

> **Blogging is a super-hero tool in encouraging the development of literacy in children of all ages.**

Blogging is a super-hero tool in encouraging the development of literacy in children of all ages. Essentially, all you are doing is modifying the parameters of who can read their work – from teachers to parents and the wider world – but this makes it incredibly powerful.

The traditional way of working looks like this:

1. Teacher sets work.
2. Child completes work in book or on worksheet.
3. Teacher marks work and provides feedback.

This simply isn't an inspiring way of working. It is the exact same way I was taught at school – things should have moved on in 20 years. So, how might blogging change this pattern?

1. Teacher sets work online – which engages children.

2. Child completes work and publishes it to blog – which creates a wider purpose for their writing and a public audience for their work, which in turn drives up the child's standards of writing and effort.

3. Teacher provides feedback – but is not the sole voice providing comments.

This new model still recognises the teacher as being an authority, in terms of subject knowledge and mastery of pedagogy, but it also allows for some of the authority over feedback to be dispersed to the wider world. This relies on you, the teacher, being able to relax the reins on your class's learning. It can be hard to relinquish total control, but in loosening up you are giving the children an authentic experience of what writing in a wider sense really means. This is so much more empowering than simply completing a worksheet. It gives the children a real voice in the world on a topic of genuine importance to them – their own learning.

Teachers and parents can be fearful of children's work being seen on the internet, but I would argue that if you have a solid grasp of e-safety – and, in particular, the children divulge no

personal information – then the anxiety over other people seeing their work is a shining example of a moral panic. So what if a stranger reads a child's essay? What bad thing could come from that?

In fact, many class blogs attract positive comments and helpful advice from all around the world. Excellent examples include David Mitchell (@DeputyMitchell) and his QuadBlogging,[1] and the 100 Word Challenge which is run by Julia Skinner (@ TheHeadsOffice), see p. 57. The big benefit of blogging is not just that you are working a different way, but that the students are growing in their confidence with the written word and sharing their ideas in a meaningful way.

There are numerous blogging platforms available, such as WordPress, Blogger and Tumblr. I use WordPress as it allows me to add students as authors and administer the content of posts. The key here is confidence, so whatever platform you choose, spend some time exploring it and making yourself aware of its positives and negatives. No one platform is perfect, so find the best fit for you and your learners.

---

1 See http://quadblogging.net/.

ONLINE PORTFOLIOS

Children can create versatile portfolios to display their work by learning to build a basic website. This can be done with very little computing skills using Weebly or Google Sites. For those over the age of 13, sites such as Pinterest or Behance can be used very effectively as visual portfolios. This would be well suited to subjects of a visual nature, such as art or DT, but it is useful to remember that they can also be used to link to other websites where more textual work is displayed. Media students, or those with a media output, can also have their own YouTube channel as long as they are over 13.

Giving students a public online space where they can curate their work not only helps to ensure that the standard of their work is high (as with blogs), but it is also excellent practice for building a positive online profile. Some universities, colleges and employers will google the name of a prospective student or employee. By putting excellent work and positive but authentic messages about themselves online, the students can get a foot in the door. This takes little more effort than creating a traditional paper-based portfolio, but it has the added benefits of being a positive advert for your student and their learning in the real world.

CONNECTING YOUR LEARNERS WITH THE REAL WORLD

One of my favourite ways to share learning is not actually dependent on the students completing a writing task. The internet gives teachers the power to connect our classrooms virtually with other classrooms around the world and with subject experts using Skype or Google Hangouts. It can be incredibly inspiring for children to speak with a class of children from another school, particularly when this can be focused on topic work or subject-specific knowledge.

Here are some ideas you could try:

- Create a debate group with another school to practise persuasive argument skills.

- Find a class in a country you have been studying to get a real insight into their culture.

- Talk with an expert or important figure who would be too busy to visit your school in person.

- Use online communication tools to work on a project around a common theme – for example, the anniversary of Magna Carta or commemoration activities surrounding the First World War. This gives children insights into how other classes or schools would view the project and exposes them to opinions and ideas beyond their own classroom. This is excellent for connecting learners with the concept that there is a world beyond what they experience every day.

- Create a maths challenge group that devises puzzles for each other to do.

- Start a cross-school business enterprise group to raise money for an agreed charity.

- Engage in some cross-faith discussions to help spread religious tolerance and cultural awareness.

- Collaborate with other local schools to solve a social problem in your area.

■ Share the children's expertise – for example, set up chats for digital leaders in different schools.

Alongside getting the children talking to each other, you could also run an email pen pal or blogging activity that will really encourage them to see themselves as citizens of the world, and not just members of your classroom.

Sharing learning is about more than just giving children an audience for their work. It is about equipping them with the digital skills they will need to be successful learners once they leave your classroom. Being a geek teacher means helping students to develop confidence in their work and believing that it has worth in the wider world. It is also about building positive relationships with parents.

TOP GEEK TIPS

■ Make sure your school's acceptable usage policy and staff guidelines are up to scratch. If needed, work with someone in your school to modernise them.

■ Choose your blogging platform carefully. Play around with a few of the options and find one that fits the needs of your learners.

■ Don't expect all teachers or parents to embrace shared online learning straightaway. Be prepared to show them why it benefits the learners.

IN THIS CHAPTER:

- How to help all learners improve their writing.
- Targeting writing skills to improve exam performance.
- Encouraging reluctant writers.

Chapter 7

WORDS

play with them, have fun with them, master them

Literacy is key to accessing the entire curriculum. Children who are unable to express their ideas on paper (and verbally), or make sense of the written word, are going to find school a very difficult place indeed. An inability to communicate can be enormously frustrating, and this is only compounded by an exam system that is almost totally geared towards the written word.[1]

There is no disputing the importance of children being able to read and write well. While I am not a specialist teacher of English, I am part of an education system that encourages every teacher to be a teacher of English. Ofsted have emphasised the need for literacy to be embedded across the curriculum, so all schools now expect it to be a focus in every subject. This chapter is about how geek teachers can help children to both express themselves and write well.

1 Many thanks to @Gwenelope and @ChocoTzar for their subject-specialist English help in this chapter.

WHY IS MASTERING WRITING SO IMPORTANT?

Many children have special educational needs. I am dyslexic myself, so having struggled through school I am always keen to support learners who have difficulties in improving their language skills. Other children have social or cultural difficulties, such as speaking English as a second language, or come from homes where reading is not cherished and encouraged. Believe me, you will have all of these children in your classroom, and you need to be able to support, encourage and improve their writing.

There has been much debate about literacy and how it should be taught in books and blogs about education. For me, language is a living thing which takes its shape and usage from the ever changing outside world. But in schools, we are often trying to marshal children into using formal language (Standard English) designed for the examination system. The two need not be at odds if you work to engender a love of writing and model the importance of writing for an audience. Watch any classroom of young children writing poems or listening to a story, and you will see a real love of the written word. Keeping that joy and focus alive as children get older is a challenge, but one that we must all rise to meet.

MAKE WRITING A HABIT

One of the best ways to improve writing is to make it a habit. I like the metaphor of training for a marathon – you wouldn't just turn up at the start line without doing any training. Extended writing is the same. You can't expect to be able to just sit down and write a 3,000 word essay.

You need to have training in how to link your ideas to the question, how to craft a conclusion and so on. All of these things need to be taught and, most importantly, practised.

So, get your class writing at every opportunity. They can write about anything – it doesn't have to be subject related.

Make the use of language non-threatening and not solely linked to formal assessment. In fact, be playful in asking them to commit pen to paper. Encourage them to write all sorts of things that won't even be read by you, such as diary entries, fortune cookie predictions, paper tweets, recipes, classroom rules, anything! Get them writing in a low-risk atmosphere so that they can experience writing as a pleasurable activity.

Teachers know that some children are frightened of writing because they have 'failed' at it before and so become reluctant to subject themselves to feeling a failure again. There is a time and a place to make writing high risk and ramp up the pressure on children to perform. However, this is a pale counterpart to nurturing them to improve.

CHALLENGE WRITING

Children can be hooked into writing by being challenged – for example, they must include X but not Y. Let's think of some ways this could be used:

- You must include descriptive adjectives but not nouns.
- You must include references to theorists but do not forget to link them to the question.
- You must include a conclusion but do not use first person.

You get the idea. Obviously you would tailor this for the subject you teach, but it is also really good practice to have several of these dos and don'ts available for students so that they can either self-differentiate and choose their own level of challenge or you give them specific tasks.

Another brilliant challenge is ask the children to write to really tight word deadlines. So, ask them to write 50 words about what they have learned. Not 49 or 51, but 50 on the nose. The process of drafting and redrafting to hit the target is a valuable skill in itself, but it also helps to develop the skills required to be able to write and edit more formally.

Alongside whole class activities, you can also have a variety of different challenges ongoing based on the same piece of learning but targeted at the individual needs of children or groups of children with similar development needs. This can be difficult to get used to at first, but my classroom is at its most productive when everyone is working on something different but still making progress in an area that is important for them.

Often children are able to point out areas of deficit in their own writing. To encourage self-evaluation, I often ask children to create their own personal learning aims, so not only will they note down the class outcome but they will also come up with one that is personal for them. It is useful to keep these in one place (e.g. the back of their books) so that they can assess if they are making progress with their self-identified targets. A half-termly review would be timely in prompting the children to maintain the momentum they have made in an area they have pinpointed as being important to them.

For less able students, or classes where you will be attempting fewer pieces of extended writing, you might consider developing a writing frame. This will help them to learn to structure their writing, as well as encourage them to write in a more analytical and evaluative way to reach the higher marks in exams.

DEVELOPING EXAM SKILLS

Often when refining writing skills teachers are focused, particularly at A level, with teaching children to write faster. After all, the aim of the exam is to write enough (in terms of quantity) to reach the top grades. However, as any teacher will tell you, written work must also be about high quality answers, not just bunging down as much as you can on the page.

Instead of focusing on writing at speed, try an activity based around slow writing.[1] Ask the children to write on double-spaced lines and to spend a predetermined amount of time writing slowly. Slowing down the pace of writing allows students to see it as more than being a rushed effort to reach the conclusion, and instead to craft each sentence. This means carefully picking each word and thinking about what punctuation they should use and the impact it might have on the meaning. Alternatively, you could slow down the writing by focusing on a different skill set or section of an essay each week. So, for example, have a dedicated week where students work on introductions, conclusions, evaluation or linking their ideas to the question. Then practise these skills in classwork and for homework.

REDRAFTING

A fantastic way to encourage students to see the value in redrafting their work, and developing their use of technical language, is to create a vocabulary grid. Choose a selection of words you want the students' to use, with a point allocation based on how tricky they are. So, for example, 'destiny' might score one point, but 'epitaph' (being a much more difficult word) would

---

1 Thanks to @LearningSpy for his thoughts on slow writing: David Didau, Revisiting Slow Writing: How Slowing Writing Might Speed Up Thinking, *The Learning Spy* (19 June 2014). Available at: http://www.learningspy. co.uk/literacy-2/revisiting-slow-writing-improving-writing-improves-thinking/.

score three. When the children have completed their written work, ask them to add up how many points they have accrued. You then give them the opportunity to edit (or totally redraft) the piece of work in order to gain more points. Children can be motivated by competition, so keep a tally chart on the board of who has the most points, or which table if you want children to compete in teams. A similar approach can be used to promote the use of key facts or phrases.

USING KEY TERMS AND DIFFERENTIATION

Another way to encourage the use of important terms and vocabulary is to make a 'chatter box' (based on an origami fortune teller). You can find editable chatter box templates on the internet, to which you can add text boxes with key terms. The learners then play with the chatter boxes (this brings on all kinds of nostalgia from when they were younger!) and use the first three terms they pick to answer a question. So, for example, when my class were revising Marxism, they wrote key terms on the flaps, such as 'capitalism', 'proletariat' and 'alienation', with the relevant definitions underneath. This is a brilliant way of reinforcing the use of technical language or vocabulary.

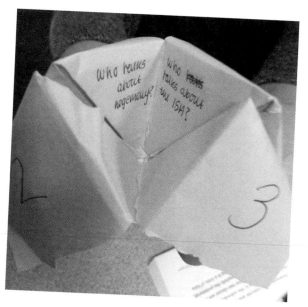

In terms of setting questions, I would consider two strategies. The first is a range of differentiated questions which allow learners either to play to their strengths and develop their confidence or to target areas for development. The second is to give the whole class one very challenging question, perhaps at the next level of study that they would find very difficult indeed (for example, when teaching A level I often set the class degree-level questions). You might think this would intimidate learners, but it can do wonders for their confidence when they successfully decode and answer a question. It also demonstrates that learning is not only hard (and worthwhile) but also that it can't always be resolved in the lesson – that there will always be something harder to think about, to learn and to accomplish. You need not be explicit about this when setting questions, but I think it is important to give a sense that learning doesn't just stop.

TAKING THE LEARNING OUTSIDE

If you feel the students would benefit from a change of scenery, then take them outdoors to practise their writing. I know that some schools do not let learning take place outside, which to my mind is a great shame. I am not advocating lolling about on the school field in the summer 'revising'. However, I feel strongly that there are a number of opportunities for learning outside the classroom walls.

One technique which is great for getting children thinking about writing is using chalk on the netball court or similar hard surface. (Remember to ask the PE staff prior to scribbling all over their courts!) Give the learners different colour chalks and space them out around the area. Each child writes on the ground a key term, piece of vocabulary or idea from the recent learning. Get them to do it nice and big. Next ask them to draw lines between each other's words and then annotate the lines with notes on how the two ideas relate to each other. This is brilliant for thinking about how ideas interconnect, and you will end up with a big chalk web as they all gradually link to each other's points. For an extra challenge you can ask them to evaluate the annotations. Being outside not only gives you the space to do this type of activity, but it also provides an almost automatic switch for engagement in the brains of most learners.

One technique which is great for getting children thinking about writing is using chalk on the netball court or similar hard surface. **(Remember to ask the PE staff prior to scribbling all over their courts!)**

**at were his major
ods of achieving
litical support?...**

→ Getting Imperium via military successes.

& Claimed to spread ancestral weight absorb powers of Senate, magistrates all into his own authority (Embrace) = Embrace

S Forced his side the Senate to marry Antony to make peace in this duels

Bribing the senate

How much political and reputational manipulation can w see in his activities

Augustus

→ Understood the power of group rule - Triumvirate etc

Ensure loyalty
|
Encouraged children to attend meetings
|
Keep Senate happy

Related to a senatorial member by blood
|
Requirements

Used Antony's scandal to gain support of senate through war
|

propaganda
re the key
cal aims.

His Expansion into mainland/west Europe — Hispania — Gaul

Major method but is manipulation

Limits the amount of

Destroys corruption

Antony's will with Cleopatra

- Garnered him same young, army by veterans at 19.
- Deserted Caesar's assassins and Antony.

Expanded his trust and influence I combined with oratory to dominate Senate and their achievements

Lack of military success in the Varus disaster

→ Rome After he Germania Augustus

is

elling hostility
provinces
|
x Romana

He returned several Powers to the senate - customs of ancestors

Created a buffer zone
|
Peace with the Parthian Empire
|
Recover the spoils of war (standards of 3 legions under Quintilius)
|
Ceremony held in Forum of Augustus
|
Battle of Philippi
|
Executed Brutus and Cassius

metal work - if we contested in war, why not in govt Parallels Churchill

**lid he use
institutions
ical roles to
his actions?**

Superior of the corn supply

He refused dictatorship and always took a college in his tribunician power to divide responsibility for his actions.

**How importa
success (hi
others) to his
governanc**

Being Caesar's heir he received title before when he controlled cities

Battle of Actium - ended Civil War - Crushed Antony's in the Mediterranean Sea

MAKING WRITING A TEAM SPORT

A fantastic way to get learners working collaboratively to improve their writing is to use a musical chairs strategy to answer an exam-style question. Start with the biggest sheets of sugar paper you can find – I like them to be different colours but you can please yourself. You will need one for every table or group of about four or five children. Write a different exam question in the centre of each sheet and give the children five minutes to mind map ideas related to it. (I always put a countdown timer on the board, and use a different one each time so it isn't too repetitious.) Instead of moving the paper from table to table, get the children to move to another table musical chairs style (I do tend to put on some music) and then ask them to critique the work of the first group, perhaps focusing on any missing knowledge content, evaluating the ideas or looking for SPaG errors. If you repeat this three times you will end up with some really quality work on the sugar paper. Then send the groups back to their original table.

Finally, ask the children to either draw up an essay plan using the information they have jointly produced or, slightly more challenging, use a mark scheme to evaluate the work they have done on the sugar paper. I'm in two minds over mark schemes. One part of me wants the students to understand exactly how the examiners will judge their work and not to oversimplify it for them. The other part of me sees that some students, particularly those of lower ability, don't fully understand complex mark schemes so it might be more appropriate for me to produce a less complex scheme. Either way, what is important is that high expectations are evident in the extension work, which should always require students to write in full sentences and hone key exam skills.

WRITING FOR YOUNGER CHILDREN (AND THE YOUNG AT HEART)

Writing for examinations aside, there are some simple ways to inspire children to write, particularly younger children. I have found that using anything apart from pen and paper is a great way to get them to practise letter shapes and start writing - be it tracing letters in sand, painting letters, writing on fabric or even in cornflour gloop.

A lot of these ideas which are so commonplace in primary settings also work well in secondary schools. Need your learners to revise? Get them to make a revision T-shirt and put on a fashion parade! Stressed sixth formers? Get them to create a massive revision mind map with paint. Children don't stop wanting to do these kinds of creative activities as they get older, and they can be a welcome break from relentless pressure around exam time.

WRITING PROMPTS

Writing prompts also work well across age groups. The best place to find suitable pictures is Pinterest. For younger children, a more indeterminate image that asks 'What is happening here?' is a fantastic way to engage them in telling a story about what might be happening. These can, of course, be linked to topic work. For older learners, the *Guardian*'s EyeWitness app has some truly amazing and sometimes harrowing images that could be linked to learning in lots of different contexts.

Having some freedom of choice in what they write about also serves to enthuse children across age groups. Story bags – cheap paper bags filled with objects, images or quotes from which learners choose a certain number to write about – can create a real excitement, not just over choosing what objects to write about but a buzz about learning and expressing that learning which never ceases to make me smile. For older children, I call these lessons a 'mystery learning tour' and totally indulge myself by playing 'Magical Mystery Tour' by the Beatles to them as they explore their bags.

Story dice can be used in a similar way. Why not ask older children to make an evaluation dice using a cube template? After making the dice, they write evaluation questions on the faces before exchanging it with a partner and writing an essay plan based on the questions they roll.

These are all brilliant ways to use unfamiliar objects to engage students in the sometimes all too familiar world of writing for a purpose or audience.

DON'T JUST WRITE ANSWERS – WRITE QUESTIONS

As well as bags and cubes, you can buy plastic eggs (again from the wonderful pound shop) and ask the children to write questions which are then popped inside the eggs. Next, arrange an egg-bombing where they throw the eggs around the room and exchange questions. Don't rush this stage: ask them to guess the question in the egg before opening the egg and going on to answer it in full sentences. This can be repeated several times. If you have been working on a specific topic area, learners are quite good at pre-empting the kind of questions that their peers might ask.

If you don't have plastic eggs, you can use paper aeroplanes or even scrunched-up sheets of paper and have a question ball fight![2] The important thing is that the resulting writing is based on peer questions about the recent learning. These activities are also valuable because they encourage the children to stand up

---

2 Thanks to @Xric32 for showing me this at #TLT.

and move about. I struggle to sit still for an hour, and so I think it is important to accept that this is going to be an issue for some of our learners. Let them move about a bit and see if their concentration improves.

Improving students' writing is crucial to classroom success. Geek teachers celebrate learners' achievements with writing and encourage them to improve. What makes children better writers is not a one-size-fits-all solution. You need to recognise that some children will need fidget toys to be able to concentrate in your lesson, while others will need to be challenged to write in a more sophisticated way using higher order thinking skills. The key is to be able to successfully differentiate by knowing the children in your classroom.

TOP GEEK TIPS

- If you are not a trained English teacher, but want to help children develop their use of language, then ask an English teacher or perhaps the literacy lead in your school for some advice.

- Keep lots of drafting paper in your classroom.

- Encourage children to write without fear of failure.

- Try writing on things other than paper – it brings out the writer in even the most reluctant child.

IN THIS CHAPTER:

- Exploring how to use IT to improve student learning.
- Building your confidence to try using new technology.
- Why using IT should never be gimmicky, or you might as well just use paper.

Let's lay this one on the line: I am not an IT zealot. I don't really understand how the internet works (magic perhaps?) and the technical side of IT is quite frankly beyond me.[1] Nor am I an Ofsted clone who thinks you need to use IT in every lesson to tick a box on a list. What I am is a trained historian and teacher who sees the genuine benefits of using technology in the classroom. IT can have a meaningful impact on the ways students learn, not just inside my classroom but outside it as well. A teacher geek knows that sometimes it can create new learning opportunities for students using technology, but that sometimes using paper is best.

---

1 Although I am working really hard to learn more!

Chapter 8

DIGITISE, ENERGISE,

but for goodness' sake stop calling yourself a 21st century practitioner

WHAT TECHNOLOGY ISN'T

Technology is not a magic bullet. Using it as a one-off to dazzle or win over your class will not work. The chances are that something will go wrong, and rather than looking like some swish lord of all things hip and cool in front of your class, you will instead look like a right berk who doesn't know why Internet Explorer is not running properly.

I have read a lot of anti-tech blogs, and they all seem (braces self to be corrected) to be written by people who don't use technology at all, or perhaps might just extend to using an overhead projector. It seems pretty easy to stand on the side lines and declare something as not being very useful, but unless you have some experience of actually trying it, or are at least willing to have a go, I'm not really sure if I'm that bothered when you declare it doesn't help children's learning.

I spend a lot of time trying things out, and quite often they don't work. But I have learned to stick with the things that do work. Some of them might be digital, and believe me there are some awesome opportunities for improving classroom learning online. But, equally, some of them will be on paper. Our students will be sitting paper exams for the foreseeable future, so training a class out of being comfortable handwriting is doing them a disservice. As educators we need to keep an eye on how students will be assessed, so we should be developing their handwriting skills as well as using IT tools that work – and occasionally innovating and trying out new things to see what we can add to our repertoire.

WHO SHOULD TEACH CHILDREN HOW TO USE TECHNOLOGY?

When using technology, the key question to keep in mind is, what benefit is it having for the student? Many schools entrust the teaching of digital skills to the IT and computing staff but, in fact, IT skills need to be taught across the whole school so that good habits can be embedded. For example, it is very common for history teachers to ask students to research and write reports that might include images. However, they need to be taught about good practice, such as using Creative Commons images and correctly crediting sources.

Some institutions have a whole school approach to literacy, but a relatively disjointed approach to IT skills. The burden of teaching children how to use PowerPoint or spreadsheets seems to fall on IT staff who have recently had the curriculum emphasis moved away from teaching ICT (i.e. students as consumers) and on to computing (i.e. students as makers of digital content). The potential fallout is that children are reaching sixth form lacking even basic IT skills.

IT is a curriculum accessing essential. It can help to develop independent thinking and is a crucial part of making children ready for higher education or work. Nothing makes me cringe more than hearing a perfectly competent learner say they are 'rubbish at computers'. I expect that maths teachers wince in the same way when they hear their subject similarly derided. Using computers isn't hard. If it was then I wouldn't have been able to teach myself how to do it simply by having a play and seeing what works.

We should expect members of staff to be competent with computers, and we should also expect students to be competent. However, too many teachers fall into the trap of expecting all children to be computer whizz-kids – the so-called 'digital natives'. Certainly, technology has permeated the lives of our young people – smartphones are ever present and anyone with a toddler will tell you, in awe, that they can use an iPad. But knowing how to use a touch screen or being au fait with Instagram does not mean that our students know how to use technology to further their learning. Be very aware of this, and give students time to work out how to use websites and apps before you start demanding work from them in a digital format.

GOOGLE APPS FOR EDUCATION

With that thought in mind, there are some digital tools that can be used to great effect across the curriculum to improve student learning, workflow and results. Without a doubt, the most powerful set of tools is Google Apps for Education (GAFE). This (depending on your admin set-up) gives students access to Google Maps, Gmail, a YouTube account, Google+ and, most importantly, Google Drive. It is really important for students to use cloud storage (in my opinion, memory sticks are the devil's work – they are easily lost, provide poor data protection and are totally ruined if a lunchbox explodes), and this suite does just that. Cloud storage is a practical step to ensure that work remains safe but is also accessible at all times. Just think, you need never hear the excuse 'It's on my memory stick' again. Joy!

Google Drive is also a very powerful sharing tool that can assist you in giving meaningful feedback. To my mind, teachers spend too much time painstakingly marking students' work, only to have the student look at the grade but give the comments very little consideration. This is not only a waste of the teacher's time, but it is also doing very little (if anything at all) to improve the student's work. Google Drive enables you to set up shared folders where you can access students' work in real time and give formative feedback whether they are working in Slides, Sheets or Docs.

Organising the settings for shared files can be tricky to set up initially, so if you are considering using the free GAFE tools then I would recommend that you get your school on board to create a school account. This will give you access to Google Classroom, which is a platform designed to integrate the Google tools into an education workflow. The main advantage for teachers is that it simplifies the sharing settings and makes creating individual or collaborative documents very easy. The advantage for students is also clear: they can have an open dialogue with their teachers about their learning and receive real time high quality feedback.

Students adapt to using GAFE very easily, and usually find that there are obvious plusses to having shared folders. The main benefit that my own students often comment on is the ability to see the work of other students. 'Hold on!' I hear you cry. 'That's cheating!' Well, no, it really isn't. Seeing other students' work actually increases transparency and pride in their individual contributions. There is no way they can copy work as everything on Google Drive is dated, so originality is relatively easily proven.

DIGITAL PEER FEEDBACK

GAFE also offers students the valuable learning opportunity to give and receive peer feedback. You can use any style of peer feedback that you feel is beneficial. The main three that I use are:

- Three stars and a wish: Ask students to say three things they like about the work and one thing that would improve it.

- Even better if … One constructive idea to make the work better.

- FISH: Friendly, insightful specific and helpful comments only.

Alongside the ability to give effective peer feedback, students can also write collaboratively. Oh, I know this sounds good but, trust me, the first few times you do it they will mess about – delete bits, type in stupid colours and generally be a bit of a nightmare. (I have delivered training to staff members on using Drive, and they do exactly the same thing!) I would give them two minutes to get this out of their system. You can have a go at managing this by dividing up the document or slides so that the students are focused on the section for which they have responsibility. As the novelty of using the tool wears off, they will stop mucking about.

The power of writing collaboratively is that students can proofread each other's work, which drives up standards of literacy across the whole class. This ethos of 'we don't just strive for our own improvement, but we improve as a team' is a powerful one, and can create a climate of learning in your classroom which will continue outside of lessons.

GOOGLE CULTURAL INSTITUTE

Alongside the GAFE tools, something else that is well worth a look is the Google Cultural Institute, which is a totally amazing bank of resources. It has three parts. The first is called World Wonders and it enables you to 'walk around' sites of historic and cultural importance – a school trip without even leaving the classroom! The second part is called Historic Moments and includes a large number of very beautiful and moving black-and-white images of key historical events. These would be fantastic writing prompts, discussion starters or images for students to use for further research. There is something very powerful about having images of such social importance concentrated in one place.

As interesting as these tools are, for me the most exciting part is the Art Project. This lets you zoom into paintings and other artworks to the extent that you can see the artist's brushstrokes – the resolution of the images is amazing. However, you can also look at the location of the artworks in galleries using Google maps. In addition, you can select images and curate them in your own gallery. This is a truly powerful tool which every teacher should make use of. It not only transforms the way that students interact with artworks, but it also introduces them to new ideas, raising their socio-cultural awareness and broadening their horizons. If it's not appropriate for your subject, then try it in tutor time.

MAKING VIDEO AND MEDIA CONTENT

There are a number of apps which are fabulous for improving student learning by enabling them to express creatively what they have learned. Apps such as Explain Everything and Shadow Puppet can be used by the students in numerous ways to make videos about their learning – for example, they could be set the task of summarising the learning that has taken place either in that lesson or over a period of time (e.g. a topic).

Another fun, and deceptively difficult, activity is to use Vine (the video version of Instagram) to make a six second summary video. Not only will the students learn how to make a stop-motion type video, but the condensed time frame of the task requires them to really think about how they communicate their learning. There are plenty of blogs and walkthrough videos that explain how to use these types of tools.

I think teachers should also be making use of video tools to provide visual/auditory feedback on students' work. If you are expecting your students to present their work as a Vine, for example, then it is only right that you provide your feedback in a similar format. This is amazingly effective when dealing with SEND learners, particularly those who have dyslexia, because they can listen to or watch the feedback more than once.

KEEPING THE LEARNERS AT THE HEART OF WHY YOU USE TECHNOLOGY

The apps you use should always be tailored to your learners. Some schools have a strict policy on the apps students can have on their devices, others push apps via mobile device management (MDM) and some will only use free apps. Whichever path you take (and your school might not even have a policy on app usage) then you need to be careful not to create a digital divide in your classroom. Bring your own device (BYOD) can be a good option, as most children have access to one device or another. (If you have a child who does not have a device then you could either have a small number of school devices than can be loaned, or ask the children to work in pairs so that those without do not feel left out or stigmatised.) You also need to be aware that not all apps will operate on all platforms, so if you set digital work then you will need to provide alternatives that can be completed using a web tool (that all children could access in the library, for example) or as a paper task.

Even if work is being produced digitally, the quality of submissions should still be high. You need to set excellent standards right from the start, and consider role modelling and sharing high quality work that you would like students to emulate. As with any written work, digital work should be persuasive and well-structured – the technology should not simply be a superficial bolt-on that takes up valuable learning time.

PODCASTING

Teachers can, of course, use apps to create flipped learning content. But, for me, digital tools are all about giving students the power to create, so why not let your students have a go at making a podcast? About five years ago I started making podcasts for students to listen to as part of their revision. It took up huge amounts of my time, and, in all honesty, they were not very good (at one point I spilt tea on myself and had to edit out some very inappropriate language). So, I started asking the students to make the podcasts instead, and the results were transformational.

As they had ownership of the material and played a key part in creating the podcast, they made really extensive use of the medium. I would advise you to use either audioBoom (which is free) or Spreaker if you want to create a more produced radio show-style broadcast. Again, quality is everything, so make sure students have a script before broadcasting and follow basic e-safety advice about not sharing personal information. You might want to consider reviewing the students' work before they post it online to avoid any unfortunate incidents or embarrassing comments. I am all about building relationships of trust, but sometimes even the nicest kids make silly mistakes and flippant comments that could be misconstrued and bring the school and yourself into disrepute.

INFOGRAPHICS

Infographics offer a brilliant way to represent data, so have obvious applications for science and maths. But they can be equally useful in teaching arts and humanities subjects, where you might ask students to interrogate statistical information – for example, the population statistics in geography or crime figures in sociology. In my experience, students who are strong in the humanities can be less comfortable working with numbers or statistical data, but they will often need to do so to succeed in their learning. Making an infographic, using a site such as Piktochart, can help to make data seem less intimidating and give students ownership over how statistics are represented and given meaning. You can save the infographics they have made, and then use ThingLink to make them interactive.

SOMETIMES THE BEST TOOL IS PAPER

Using digital tools can be a double-edged sword. They can generate curiosity and interest in the learning or they can make the lesson overcomplicated and gimmicky. Trust your professional judgement. As a hook for learning, digital tools can be effective in a way that pen and paper can't, but I also think that paper can be simply magical too. The very best teachers are able to blend analogue and digital tools to suit the needs of their learners, although the confidence to exploit IT has to be learned over time.

Don't be wary of the learning process: by learning and developing your skills you are role modelling being a learner to your class – you are being the thing that you want them to be.

And this means accepting that lessons using IT might not always go smoothly (although the same can also apply to lessons without IT!). You are an awesome teacher, and you are going to have all kinds of exciting impact in your classroom by giving both old and new technologies a go.

FOR SLT

It has come as quite a shock to some senior leaders that the internet is not a passing fad. Facebook has not gone away; Twitter is still going strong; Instagram is stubbornly persisting (although Myspace has died a death). Not only is the internet here to stay, but it has become an everyday communication tool like nothing else we have ever seen. Imagine how many postcards would need to be sent, or carrier pigeons dispatched, to match the number of tweets sent per day.

Education has fallen behind remarkably quickly – indeed, lots of us are actually deskilling students by taking their mobile devices out of their hands. Yes, young people need to learn to read and write and add up using pens and paper. Yes, they will be examined using these traditional methods. But if one of the purposes of education is to prepare students for the world of work, then it could be argued that we're not preparing them at all – even restaurant waiting staff are now using iPads.

Senior leaders are well aware that a great deal of their pastoral leaders' time is taken up dealing with the fall-out from inappropriate social media use. Pictures are sent, insults are traded, threats are made, friends get involved, rumours persist … and the school day is disrupted.

So, why would geek teachers encourage the use of digital devices in lessons? Because the bad mouthing and insults are a behaviour issue not a technology issue. Because students need to learn about good protocols for using devices in school and in the wider world. (They need to learn that harmful words exist in the real world too and have real consequences.) Because we never banned exercise books and pens when students tore out pages and sent notes to one another in class. Because they need to know that there is more power in their hands than simply Google and Flappy Birds. But mostly because the opportunities for learning are huge.

Head teachers – please embrace digital technology. Do not blindly ban devices without considering the positives. Work with your digital advocates to create policies that will work and encourage the responsible and proactive use of new technologies.

TOP GEEK TIPS

- Always check out a web tool or app you are going to use in advance of lessons.
- Keep in mind that the cost of apps can add up, so some schools opt to use only free ones.
- Don't rely on your learners to digitally store their work – they need to be trained to do this like Pavlov's dogs!

Conclusion

Maybe it's the way I have been taught to write, but I think everything should have a conclusion – even a book that wants to challenge conceptions about what we should do in education. My children are both currently Harry Potter obsessed, and so I shall take some inspiration from J. K. Rowling and 'open at the close'.[1]

I asked you at the beginning of this book if you were feeling brave, and if you would be prepared to rethink some of your practice to improve the teaching and learning in your classroom. Remember, this is about using techniques that you already use or that already exist and doing something new with them. Putting a new spin on things. Thinking differently. Being yourself in your teaching but from a new perspective. I hope you now feel inspired to be a little more adventurous, and are seeing the opportunities that being a geek teacher could provide your students.

Finally, I would like you to think about these six points when you are planning lessons, teaching in the classroom or marking students' work:

1. **It is easier to ask for forgiveness than permission.** By this I don't mean do something ridiculous that will get you suspended or featured in the local press. If you are trying something new, remember you are a competent professional – you don't always need to seek approval from those around or above you.

   Ideas that have real merit and stickability are the ones that are focused on the children in your classroom, or the children on whom you can have a positive impact. Don't ever lose sight of this – be it for observations or when planning your lessons.

2. **Pursue new activities in your classroom.** Be OK with taking risks and brave enough to call it when they are not working out.

---

1 J. K. Rowling, *Harry Potter and the Deathly Hallows* (London: Bloomsbury, 2007).

You are the professional in the room. You are in charge of what goes on there. You are accountable to your class and yourself. Also remember to be kind to yourself. If an idea doesn't work, allow yourself some time to reflect on what went wrong. This doesn't mean the idea doesn't work at all, just that it wasn't successful this time.

3. **Seek out opportunities to work with others and try to say yes as often as possible to opportunities that come your way.** Teach this open-mindedness to your students too.

Being an isolated professional in a classroom is not much fun. It can sap your love of your job and make every day seem more difficult than it needs to be. However, you are not alone: through other teachers you can find support, nurturing and share/exchange ideas. This can be done through your own or another local school, a national or subject organisation or social media. However you do it, I urge you to get involved. There is an exciting and vibrant teaching community beyond your classroom walls. We can all learn from each other, even if some of what we learn is that certain ideas and techniques are not for us, or that we should aim to grow our own self-confidence.

4. **Use technology where appropriate.** Accept that it won't always work and be comfortable with your students being more skilled than you.

Drop any idea about children being digital natives and invest time and energy into demonstrating the positive use of new technologies. Remember, using an iPad or app can be exciting and inspiring, but so can using a pen and paper. It is not the case that one is better than the other, so use your judgement to decide which one will provide the best path to the best learning outcomes.

5. **Don't accept the view that good pedagogy is constrained by subject or age.** Some of the most inspiring teaching practice I have seen has been in the primary phase, but it adapts perfectly well for use in secondary and beyond.

There is so much true here it hurts. We might also look to professional practice in universities and educational research to inform our ideas and practice. The key is not to pigeonhole ideas because they originated from someone who teaches different age children to you. Quite frankly, that is daft.

6. **Be yourself.** Share some of yourself with your class. You are not a teaching robot; you are a human being. Know your learners and plan with them at the centre of everything.

    Remember, too, the importance of switching off from work and loving your own family and giving them the same care and attention as you do the children in your class. Caring for them and yourself is vital.

Success for me isn't simply measured in terms of examination results; it is in the difference we can make to the lives of those in our classrooms. My very favourite *Doctor Who* quote is, 'Nine hundred years of time and space and I've never met anybody who wasn't important before.'[2] I always think, in 13 years of teaching I have never met a child who wasn't important or whose life I could not have a positive impact on. We are all of us – teachers, parents and children – important in our educational community. As professionals, we should celebrate our inner teacher geek, as the passion and drive to help children achieve will go a long way to making a real difference.

---

2 'A Christmas Carol', *Dr Who* (BBC), 25 December 2010.

Resources

LEARNING TOOL WEBSITES

www.100wc.net

www.abandoned-places.com

www.aurasma.com

www.behance.net

www.bimadday.org.uk

www.blackoutpoetry.net

www.bluethirst.co.uk

www.childnet.com

compfight.com

www.google.com/culturalinstitute

www.google.com/hangouts/

www.instagram.com

www.nearpod.com

Piktochart.com

www.pinterest.com

quadblogging.net

www.skype.com

www.socrative.com

www.soundbible.com

www.swgfl.org.uk

www.thinglink.com

www.tumblr.com

www.twitter.com

www.vimeo.com

https://vine.co

www.weebly.com

www.wordpress.org
www.youtube.com
www.zippcast.com

LEARNING TOOL APPS

audioBoom

Aurasma

Explain Everything

GarageBand

Google

Grafio

Guardian Eyewitness

Over

Piktochart

Spreaker